Setting Boundaries

How to Set Boundaries With Friends, Family, and in Relationships, Be More Assertive, and Start Saying No Without Feeling Guilty

Linda Hill

Linda Hill

© Copyright 2022 - Linda Hill - All rights reserved.

The content contained within this book may not be reproduced, duplicated or transmitted without direct written permission from the author or the publisher.

Under no circumstances will any blame or legal responsibility be held against the publisher, or author, for any damages, reparation, or monetary loss due to the information contained within this book, either directly or indirectly.

Legal Notice:

This book is copyright protected. It is only for personal use. You cannot amend, distribute, sell, use, quote or paraphrase any part, or the content within this book, without the consent of the author or publisher.

Disclaimer Notice:

Please note the information contained within this document is for educational and entertainment purposes only. All effort has been executed to present accurate, up to date, reliable, complete information. No warranties of any kind are declared or implied. Readers acknowledge that the author is not engaged in the rendering of legal, financial, medical or professional advice. The content within this book has been derived from various sources. Please consult a licensed professional before attempting any techniques outlined in this book.

By reading this document, the reader agrees that under no circumstances is the author responsible for any losses, direct or indirect, that are incurred as a result of the use of the information contained within this document, including, but not limited to, errors, omissions, or inaccuracies.

Linda Hill

Table of Contents

Your Free Gift 1

Introduction 3

    A Few Mentions 6

Chapter 1: Understanding Boundaries 16

    Why You Need Boundaries 16

    Healthy Boundaries 19

    Your Personal Boundaries 26

    No Boundaries 45

    Journaling 49

Chapter 2: Boundary Myths 52

    Boundary Myths and Reconsiderations 54

    Always Saying "No" 90

Journaling 100

Chapter 3: How to Be More Assertive 101

Strategies for Assertiveness with Boundaries 102

Combating Assertion Guilt 114

Combating Your Weaknesses 115

Journaling 126

Chapter 4: Setting Boundaries in Relationships 129

Extenuating Circumstances 129

Setting Boundaries With Family Members 134

With Friends 154

Setting Boundaries in Romantic Relationships 155

At Work 158

Online 162

Journaling 163

Chapter 5: Life With Boundaries 165

Confronting the Ignorant 166

What Goes Around Comes Around 168

Conclusion 169

Thank You 171

References 173

Your Free Gift

As a way of saying thanks for your purchase, I want to offer you a free bonus e-Book called How to Say "No", exclusive to readers of this book.

In this book you'll discover:

- How to say "no" without feeling guilty or hurting other's feelings

- How to quit people pleasing and stand up for yourself
- How to distinguish between being a helpful person and being a doormat
- And so much more

If you finally want to end people pleasing for good, then grab this book.

To get instant access, just go to:

PeakPublishBooks.com/people

Or Scan the QR Code below:

Introduction

Understanding and using personal boundaries is a lot harder than one would think. Today, many people are aware of the concept of personal boundaries, including the need to enforce them constantly within all types of relationships. But the heart of boundaries, and one of the reasons why it is so important to have and maintain them is often forgotten: Your boundaries are actually a form of self-care.

It might sound funny, but it is true. Self-care includes your subconscious and your inner emotions. Boundaries are essentially the understanding of what you are willing to be responsible for, or not (Cloud & John Sims Townsend, 2002). Note that the actual definition will be more fully stated in the next chapter, but for now, let's get this foundation of knowledge started. You have almost the perfect formula for a form of self-care, which will protect your interests while helping you maintain healthy relationships and a holistic life-balance.

Some of you may be wondering why the beginning of this book is highlighting the connection between boundaries and self-care. Because this is arguably one of the most important forms of self-care to be practiced daily, yet it is most often the one that is constantly ignored.

But... Why are boundaries and their care ignored?

Primarily, because of the bad reputation boundaries have gotten. People are often hesitant to enact their own boundaries because they are afraid of the freedoms they will be taking away from other people, or, they have been led to feel guilty over standing up for their boundaries.

A great way to combat these feelings is by labeling your boundaries as a form of self-care. The minute you begin to reframe your boundaries as something you need to

Introduction

maintain for your own good—and something to ensure that you are at your best to be present in your overall life—it is much easier to stand up for them and ensure that they are maintained in the long term.

Additionally, giving them this label will help begin to remove one of the biggest 'problems' with setting and enforcing boundaries: That we often feel guilty for doing so.

While this will be covered in later chapters, this is something that needs to be addressed right here and now: Setting a boundary is nothing to feel guilty about. It is normal, natural, and a sign that you are creating a healthy relationship. Yes, knowing these things will not make the guilt go away instantly. In fact, it is something that you are going to have to actively fight for a long time while figuring out your boundary journey. However, it does get easier. Eventually, setting and enforcing your boundaries will cause a lot less guilt and will actually—believe it or not—create relief.

So trust in the process, and trust that you are doing the right thing for yourself. Because you are.

A Few Mentions

How to Use the Book

Before going any further, it is important to note the actual structure of how this book is written, and how it will apply to you.

In this book, we will discuss boundaries, boundary myths, how to be more assertive, and how to set and enforce your own boundaries. There will be scenarios and examples which will be used to specifically show where things went wrong, or how certain things could work. While reading these examples, keep your journal close so that you can write down what similarities you have, what you think will work, and what you need to think on. These scenarios will try to cover as many concepts as possible, but since boundaries are an incredibly personal and individual concept, it will be important for you to really think and analyze your own situation before going ahead and enacting any of the recommendations.

Journaling

As mentioned above, having a journal can be considered a companion to this book. When it comes to figuring out your personal boundaries, why some of your boundaries may not be met, and how you are going to enforce them in your own life, journaling is going to be a key component of helping to keep your thoughts straight. You can use a hand-written journal, or something like your phone, tablet, computer, or even an audio recording device, to keep your thoughts and concepts safe.

For this journey, writing down your thoughts will be a key element in helping you isolate the qualities of the boundaries you have—because we all have them—and begin to expand and more strongly identify the specifics of those boundaries. It is only once we actually sit down and begin to analyze certain scenarios and emotions, that we are able to isolate and give phrases to the boundaries we need to express the most.

Additionally, journaling through the examples and how they correlate to your own situations will help you begin to discern what methods and considerations will work best for you and your situation.

Terms

In this book there will be several terms used, which may be self-explanatory; but just in case, they will be described here and can be referred to as you go.

Safe People

The term "safe people" has been around for years, but the problem is that so often—like boundaries—it is not well defined. So, that will be done now. Safe people are people who we can connect with on a deeper level, who are able to tell us the truth in a way where we hear and understand them, and who allow us to be human, while also expecting and helping us become a better person (Cloud & John Sims Townsend, 2022/1995). In other words, safe people are the ones that you feel you can tell anything to. They are the sounding board of wisdom and are the ultimate veto-power of knowledge which you trust. These people also call you to a higher standard of yourself. Sure, they will laugh and joke with you, but at the end of the day, if you are doing something questionable, they will call you out on it.

Safe people are also those with whom we have a deep connection. It is not really recommended to make a safe person out of someone you just met. Would you take the advice of someone you just met in spin class on a very personal or sensitive subject? That is not to say that those types of relationships may not become safe people over time, but that should not be the immediate case.

Safe People and Boundaries

So, why do you need safe people? Well, when you look at the definition of what they do for our lives, they are honestly indispensable regardless of where you are on your mental health, or boundaries, journey. However, when it comes to enacting, enforcing, and even thinking about what your boundaries are, a safe person is a great sounding board to bounce ideas off of. Since they know you pretty well, and are already someone who can call you out on those interesting scenarios, they may have a good inclination of certain areas that need, or need better, boundaries.

That does not mean you need to go to them explicitly for advice. However, if you have certain areas or boundary ideas that you are unsure of, these are great people to go to.

Small Note

Yes, there will be many of these in this book, so might as well get used to them now. Therapists, psychologists, and counselors are the only people who can be safe people almost immediately. Why? Because that is what they are trained to do. As long as you have done your homework (e.g.,, made sure of what university they went to, how long they have been practicing, and looked up reviews), it is pretty much guaranteed that, outside of something that would be the next Hollywood special, these people are safe. They will guide you through this process as well. So do not be afraid to reach out to one if you think you need that level of help.

The Flags

These may be terms that are a little outdated, but generally the flags are used like the traffic light system,

Introduction

and can be used in personal relationship assessments as well as emotional responses to the world around you.

When it comes to boundaries, the flags can be used in two ways: First, you can use them to help assess your emotional responses to someone else's boundaries, your boundaries, your feelings in a situation, etc., like: "*I got angry when so-and-so told me I couldn't come over again tonight. How do I feel about this situation? Am I happy to leave them be, or am I pushing their established boundaries?*"

Second, the flags can be used to identify how certain people react to the performance of your boundaries, like: "*My friend was furious when I told him I needed some space. He said I didn't care about him at all, and if I did, I'd put my feelings aside for his. Which flag would I give to their reaction to my boundaries?*"

Red Flag

Similar to red lights, *red flags* are things you have noticed in a relationship that are a problem. But this is not just something you note and move on from, these are the "stop immediately and leave," types of problems. For instance, if there is abuse, duplicity, or deceit. In relation to boundaries, a red flag is equal to an unsafe person, or someone who does not respect your boundaries. These people may be well-meaning, but they will never be respectful and will always push. For those types of scenarios it is up to you on what to do, and honestly, on the level of boundary (which will be covered in the first chapter) that they are ignoring. If it is a big boundary (like sexual or physical consent) then find a safe person, or mediator, and end that relationship, or put very strict guidelines on it.

Red flags are the warning signs, and if you are noticing lots of red flags, get help and make sure you tell a safe person about it to stop any potential backlash. Additionally, a safe person can be a neutral third-party who can help you figure out logistics on how to get out.

Yellow Flags

In comparison to red flags, yellow flags are where things are more up to personal discretion. The reason for this is because yellow flags tend to either become red flags (big problem) or green flags (it resolves itself). Now, it is important to note that if a yellow flag becomes a red flag, listen to the advice in the above section and get out. However, for the most part, yellow flags tend to be scenarios where you can either wait and see how it goes, or avoid that situation altogether. This is mainly because yellow flags tend to be either phases of life (e.g., jobs, finances, etc.), or integral problems within yourself or others that you or the other person are willing to fix.

When it comes to boundaries, yellow flags are often when something needs to be addressed, but then is resolved through open communication and understanding.

If you are still unsure if something is a yellow flag, a great way to figure it out is by talking with the person where the yellow flag has popped up. If they are open to resolution, then the situation was a yellow flag which turned into a green flag. If they are not willing to resolve, then it is a red flag and you can consult the above section on what to do.

Green Flags

Compared to red and yellow, green flags do not really need an explanation, but a brief one will be given just in case. Green flags are the things that are great, perfect, or workable in a relationship. Ergo, they do not need work or any type of conflict resolution.

Small Note

It is normal for relationships to have a mixture of yellow and green flags, and since boundaries are a form of relationships, the same can be said for that. The big thing to notice when it comes to boundaries compared to relationships, is that yellow flags in response to boundaries—or as a boundary—should be resolved immediately, instead of waiting for them to resolve themselves.

General Note for This Book

Something that really needs to hit home before continuing, is that this book aims to help you understand and implement your own boundaries. However, boundaries are a personal responsibility as well as a personal choice, as you will see in the next chapter where the definition of boundaries are given. Therefore, there may be times in your own life during

Introduction

very specific instances or events, where implementing your boundaries may be tricky, and a bit more nuanced than what you may be comfortable with on your own.

If this ever happens to you, go to your safe person or to a licensed therapist and ask for clarification. Just with any type of new emotion-based habit, there will be times when your boundaries are a bit confusing, or do not make a lot of sense. That is nothing to be ashamed of, and asking for help is not a waste of money or time—as long as you go to the right person—because they will help you understand the specifics of your situation and how to handle them.

Chapter 1

Understanding Boundaries

As with learning anything new, understanding what you are going to learn about is the first step. Here are a few ways to begin understanding boundaries. Specifically, in this chapter, we will talk about concepts like why you *need* boundaries, and what healthy and unhealthy boundaries look like.

Why You Need Boundaries

To start us off is the question, "Why do we need boundaries?" The answer is found in the definition. According to Doctor Henry Cloud, boundaries are simply the difference between what is yours, and what is not yours (Cloud & John Sims Townsend, 2002). This applies to everything from tasks to emotions to time to finances. So then, if the answer is so simple, why is it so hard to define, live out, and even understand why they are needed?

Because real life is messy and more importantly, society often has different opinions of what is our problem versus what are other's problems. Yet, when we think of boundaries in a different way, it is pretty easy to begin defining what is yours versus what is someone else's.

Try the following exercise: Every time you consider a boundary, think of it like your personal property line. Most people are highly aware—and even make it their duty—to determine what is their responsibility versus someone else's (like a neighbor or the municipal government) when it comes to their homes. If you begin to think of boundaries in a simple black and white landscape like home ownership, figuring out what is your personal boundary versus someone else's can become a bit easier.

So What Is the Problem?

This is going to sound repetitive—so prepare yourself—but the problem with boundaries and enacting them often comes down to what people are willing to be responsible for, or not. Boundaries involve a deep amount of personal responsibility, as well as personal recognition and freedom. For instance, it would be so easy to say that your happiness is defined by someone else and their actions; and while that may have a smidge of truth—like how the actions of that person will help influence how happy you are in one particular moment. That generalization of making your happiness a byproduct of someone else's actions, and therefore their responsibility, is a poor boundary, and a good way to ensure that you are never happy.

See the problem? Unfortunately, if you are one of those people who would prefer for their innermost happiness and peace to be defined by others, you are not going to have the best of times with the rest of this book. Good news is, though, that you will be given tools and examples to help realize where you might be implicating that habit, and how to stop it.

What Boundaries Are

Which brings us to what your boundaries actually *are*. As previously mentioned, boundaries are essentially what you are willing/should be responsible for in your own life. This includes your emotions, your responsibilities, your actions, and how you are going to handle relationships.

Healthy Boundaries

Healthy boundaries are what we are striving for. So then, what is a healthy boundary? Easy. Healthy boundaries are boundaries you are willing to enforce—and do consistently—which help your overall being live up to its fullest potential. They encompass everything that you should and are willing to be responsible for in each area of your life, and they have been healthily communicated to those in close contact with you, and you have ensured that they are flexible enough to weather any scenario that comes your way.

Yes, it sounds like a lot—and to be completely honest,

it is a lot of work to set up and maintain in the beginning—but it will bring infinite happiness and relief for the rest of your life, so the work and due diligence will be worth it.

In sum, healthy boundaries are the complete understanding and enforcement of your own boundaries in every scenario, no matter how big or small; and in every scenario where they are healthily communicated, your boundaries are respected and acknowledged.

Big and Small Boundaries

Which brings about something to begin thinking about now: the difference between big and small boundaries. First of all, each of these types of boundaries are important; the size of your personal boundaries should never have any effect on what you insist other people respect in their interactions with you. The sizing term allocated to these boundaries are really used as a type of emotional marker to help you better organize how you can/should respond to the violation of those boundaries.

Big Boundaries

Big boundaries are the important, non-negotiables that should never be crossed. If a larger boundary is crossed, that is a red flag, deal breaker, the neon red sign that something is wrong in the relationship or circumstance. Why is it such a big deal? Because big boundaries are important things like consent, transparency, and respect that you have with the other individual or individuals, depending on the scenario.

Would you really be okay if someone ignored your consent? Would you really be okay if your partner cheated on you? Would you really be okay if your family lied to you and stole all your money?

Most likely the answer to all of those questions was a big fat 'no', and it should be.

These types of boundary violations are significant, mainly because these boundaries are the life-altering issues that thankfully most societies still intrinsically protect and enforce. There is a big chance that you are not even sure what all of your big boundaries are, and that is okay.

Think about whatever is a dealbreaker to you in any scenario. If you suddenly feel: unsafe, unwanted, or like there is a big problem, that scenario is first of all dangerous—so get out and get somewhere safe and contact someone safe. But also, that scenario is the destruction of a big boundary.

Small Boundaries

In comparison, a small boundary could be simply when someone is rude to you in a store. This type of boundary is something that is expected, and generally enforced by good manners or social etiquette. However, when they are crossed, you have the ability to either ignore it and be fine with that small slight, or be able to confront the person without too much backlash or drama (hopefully) in the physical setting. So, for the example of someone being rude to you in a store, you have the option of either ignoring and going about your day with only a few negative thoughts as you walk away, or the ability to confront them with something mild, such as: "I do not deserve your rudeness." Unless you do, in which case, you really need to start considering how you treat service workers.

Small Note

The dismissal of your smaller boundaries is not something to scoff at; in fact, many people are justifiably annoyed when those are ignored. However, in many societies, these are the small slights which could begin to be perceived as 'petty' or not being able to let certain things go. And that is wrong. No matter how big or small your boundaries are, they should be respected and not deliberately crossed. The problem is with how we communicate and react to those boundaries being ignored.

If you get annoyed at your small boundaries being crossed, that is not something to be ashamed of. That is a healthy response and not something you should let other people belittle you for. However, if your reactions to those boundaries being crossed are disproportionate, then you should take a moment right now and mark down in your journal why these small slights cause such a large reaction.

Often, when our reactions are larger than the actual scenario, something is building behind the scenes in our subconscious, and it is that particular build-up which is inadvertently coming out. And it is this build-up that we want to address and begin to take down.

Boundaries Can Be Fluid

Part of breaking down that subconscious and/or internal build-up of boundaries being crossed is beginning to understand that some boundaries can be fluid. Your boundaries are built from your beliefs, understandings, and background. What this means is that some of your small boundaries—and even your big ones—may change to accommodate or acknowledge your past or new knowledge. That is okay, and honestly, that is what we want for some of them.

That does not mean that you should change your boundaries for every new person or circumstance, but that also does not mean that you should maintain an old boundary if it is now harmful to you. And for some of us, it is understanding this difference which can cause a lot of disproportionate responses to our boundaries being crossed.

For example, say that you previously lent out money to friends relatively willingly, within reason. Then, over time, you began to notice that people were taking advantage of that generosity and were not respecting your own financial goals and situations. You then alter your previous boundary, but still helped out one particular friend who desperately needed the help due to recently losing their job during a volatile life situation.

In the above example, you altered your boundaries in response to a pre-existing boundary not being respected. However, at the same time, you were able to maintain an understanding and flexibility to help out the friend who really needed your help. This is what boundary fluidity means, and beginning to understand and enact that type of fluidity will most likely help you begin to lose the constant feeling of annoyance which lurks beneath the surface.

Your Personal Boundaries

Now that you know what healthy boundaries are, it is time to begin applying that knowledge to yourself. Your boundaries are based on your integral beliefs, what you are or are not willing to do, values, opinions, and perspectives (Blundell, 2019).

What this also means is that your boundaries can be influenced and change depending on life circumstances, traumas, or learning lessons you encounter along the way (Blundell, 2019). Good news is that it means that while some of your boundaries may be more permanent than others, they are not necessarily life-long commitments or decisions you have to immediately make.

If you are struggling with how to begin thinking about your boundaries, take a moment and ask yourself these three questions: "What is 'me'?" or, "What is not 'me'?" and, "What do I 'own' and take responsibility for, versus what will I not?" (McLaughlin, 2000). Seriously, take a moment with your handy journal and begin to write down the answers to those questions.

Make sure you do this, because those answers are actually the foundations of your boundaries.

What Your Boundaries Look Like

Now that you are beginning to have a vague idea of what your boundaries may be, it is time to see what your boundaries may actually look like—the phrasing to describe them and the understanding of what your boundaries are. Intrinsically, boundaries exist in every scenario we encounter and thankfully, they are often categorized as such. For instance, the boundaries you have at home versus at work probably have some differences. However, beginning to separate and differentiate boundaries becomes tricky.

First of all, differentiating and categorizing your boundaries becomes problematic because a lot of these areas overlap. For instance, many of us have physical, financial, and time based boundaries, like the work/life balance, consent on romantic dates or with family members, not lending out more than 'x' amount of money at a time, etc.). But as you can see in the parenthesis, certain things like the difference between work and life begin to mesh themselves into the abstract boundary of 'time'.

Good news is that these first scenario boundaries are all good definitions of firm boundaries. Sure, they may be subject to change depending on circumstances, but for the most part, these are pretty steadfast rules that you are willing to live by, and will consistently enforce no matter the scenario. You merely have to begin teasing them out of your subconscious mind.

When it comes to setting these more firm boundaries, take a look at areas in your life which matter the most, such as: physical, sexual, emotional, financial, and intellectual (Pattemore, 2021). These are all big concepts of your life, which transcend company like family, friends, romance, and work.

Before you get overwhelmed on how to begin defining your boundaries in each of these areas, think of it this way: You are looking for situations where you give an immediate and hearty 'no' in response to the situation. For every 'no' that you come up with, you have a boundary.

For instance, if you get upset when someone dismisses your thoughts or opinions immediately, without elaborating or discussing them with you (even if that means to help you better understand), then that is an intellectual boundary you have.

Now, this is where boundaries get tricky, because they concern the basic understanding of your responsibility versus others reactions and their own responsibility towards you; plus the ever so difficult circumstance of healthily communicating your boundaries appropriately (if this concerns you, do not worry, we will get there). A good rule of thumb when it comes to your own boundaries is that boundaries and communication go together like popcorn and butter, or peanut butter and jelly, or whatever other food combination you absolutely cannot do without. As long as you communicate your boundaries in a clear and precise way, without being rude, you are in the clear.

For instance, say that you have a pretty firm physical boundary of not hugging people unless they are immediate family. When you meet a friend of a friend, you notice that they are hugging everyone in the circle. Unconcerned, when it comes to your turn to be introduced, you smile and politely say "I do not hug other people, but I am glad to meet you." In this example, you are not being rude to the new person you are meeting, you are being firm and friendly over a personal boundary you are not willing—and honestly should not have to—compromise (Campbell, 2021).

Expressing your boundaries does not have to be painful, conflict-based, or even something to feel anxiety over (although you might the first few times, and that is perfectly okay if you are not accustomed to setting or enforcing your boundaries). It will get easier as you go along, and remember: your personal boundaries are yours alone.

Your Boundaries, Your Happiness

It may seem a little too good to be true, but there you have it. Your boundaries—and yours alone—will ensure that you are happy in the long run.

Understanding, enforcing, and even adapting them, will help you maintain a strong sense of self, as well as help you keep an inner eye on what you need or want, in any given scenario. However, this type of happiness and personal freedom does not come easily, or even immediately. It will take a lot of hard work and persistence to ensure that you maintain this happiness. Over time, this work will become easier—and perhaps even automatic in some scenarios—but be forewarned: it will require an adjustment period to get there.

It is important to remember that you are setting your boundaries for yourself. No one else. You are not setting these boundaries for your friends, your partner, your family, or even your children or dependents. Yes, they will benefit from you setting them, but they are not *for* them. They are for you.

You, Your Boundaries, and Your Emotions

Boundaries and emotions have a strong bond, particularly because we display our emotions when our boundaries are crossed.

Think about it this way: When you get annoyed at something, there is some sort of action or scenario which triggers those emotions. A majority of the time, when we feel a negative emotion but are unsure why, it is because some type of boundary or particular protocol that we as individuals inherently follow, has been crossed. But this particular protocol is not something which is universally acknowledged or understood, which then means that anytime it is disrespected we are faced with two options: to either let it pass, or to somehow deal with the emotions that are now triggered.

The problem is that as adults, we are taught to ignore or not display those emotions, especially over small slights. Which honestly, is not healthy and slightly wrong. Yes, as adults, we should probably not have a massive meltdown in the grocery store every time we do not get the cookie. Mainly because—we *are* adults, we can buy the cookie if we really, really want too. But being frustrated at the reasons as to why you probably should not buy the cookie, such as: you are trying to not eat as much sugar, you already have other cookies in your cart, you do not have the money for it this month, etc., are completely valid. Any of those reasons would be more than enough to be annoyed that you cannot buy what you want at that particular moment. However, just because you are annoyed is not an excuse to then disrupt everyone else's life and day by throwing a massive fit in the middle of the store. And for the most part, the majority of adults do know that. The social niceties and expectations have become ingrained in us over time—which is partly why the outliers who do not acknowledge or understand these niceties—are so harshly ostracized.

Which then brings us back to our boundaries and emotions. When our boundaries are crossed, negative emotions will arise, and how we respond and display those emotions are where the true work behind enforcing our own boundaries while respecting others will come into play.

Before going any further, there is something you should know: Your emotions are always valid.

Being frustrated that you cannot buy, do, or react the way you want is completely normal and arguably healthy. However, it is how you display those emotions where inappropriate behaviors and mindsets can occur. It is also in this sphere where boundaries come into play. Being upset that a boundary was disrespected is completely valid; in fact, that upset is even encouraged, because you need to understand the 'why' attached to your emotions (i.e.: your boundary being destroyed). However, if you were to disproportionately display those negative emotions, you begin to escalate a situation way beyond what it was meant to be (depending on the situation, obviously). More in-depth scenarios will be given in later chapters, but what is vital to understand here is that understanding the 'why' behind some of your emotions will help you begin to identify certain boundaries that are important to you, and are most likely the ones you should address first.

Being able to self-monitor your own emotions is a grueling task, but the rewards—especially in regards to boundaries—are endless. For instance, you will be able to better pinpoint why certain emotions are being triggered, how to calm yourself down, and also have a better understanding of how certain scenarios are toxic and/or triggering for you and how to fix or avoid them in the future. Additionally, understanding how your boundaries were crossed will give you an amazing stepup in combating how to communicate your boundaries to those around you, to ensure a healthier space for you and everyone else.

You, Your Boundaries, and Others

Which then brings up the ever so fun discussion of how your boundaries work with other people. In this section, we are going to cover a basic understanding, as in-depth relationships will be discussed in a different chapter.

In sum, you need to understand that everything we are doing here, is for your own boundaries, and that these boundaries are yours and yours alone. That is it. That is all. They. Are. Yours.

What this also means is that how people respond to them is intrinsically not your problem. If someone reacts poorly, while that is really unfortunate, that is not your fault.

Your Boundaries, Your Responsibility

Now, this is not an indication for you to say, "Yes, I know, they are mine," and leave it at that; your boundaries are your own responsibility. It is no one else's job to give you your boundaries, to uphold your boundaries, or to even necessarily know your boundaries.

Discovering, enforcing, and continuing your boundaries is your job, and yours alone. Yes, people and experiences can help you shape certain boundaries which you will continue to uphold, and you can always go to safe people, a therapist, or even a knowledgeable trusted friend (but be careful with that one), to help you define, understand, or even figure out what your boundaries are or should be. This is in no way saying that you need to find your boundaries completely on your own, or that you should not even take certain people's perspective into consideration.

What it means is that while there are hopefully a group of people to help you on this journey, figuring out and displaying your boundaries will ultimately live and die with you. Your friends can respect them, and even help remind you of them in the beginning if you need them too, but at the end of the day they will not feel the same level of upset, hurt, or frustration, when your boundaries are crossed. Their lives will go on, and their other relationships will remain relatively unaffected by your boundaries not being enacted or respected.

However, the same cannot be said for you.

On this journey of discovering your own boundaries, you need to recognize that you are personally responsible to yourself and others around you, for your end of the bargain.

Most relationships work on a relative understanding of the other's boundaries. For instance, most relationships go through the "what are we" talk where certain boundaries and expectations are discussed and set; and it is pretty clear that if any of those terms are violated, the relationship will be in danger. Apply that principle of setting boundaries clearly and succinctly in the other relationships in your life as well, and enact that level of responsibility.

Boundaries and Communication

Yes, the above statements are all true: You should act and protect your boundaries when necessary, and you should definitely be on the lookout for when your boundaries are not being met or are flat-out being ignored. However, what this also means is that you have to be aware of your own personal responsibility to yourself and others around you. People can only respect or ignore a boundary that is explicitly stated and understood by everyone in the conversation or scenario. So, if you have boundaries, but do not share them with those that you interact with on a daily basis, you cannot be completely upset when those boundaries are ignored.

Before that tangent gets out of hand: The above statement is in no way absolving when someone ignores your lack of consent, refuses to understand or attempts to understand you when you communicate boundaries to them, or when a bully truly does not care about them. What the above statement specifically points out is that in order for you to have the freedom that personal boundaries give, you have to be willing to be held accountable to the responsibility of enforcing them on a daily basis; specifically, communicating them constantly.

For instance, say that you became mad with your friend because they told something you had mentioned to them—in confidence—to mutual friends. If you had not explicitly told your friend that the nugget of information was confidential, it would not necessarily be that friend's fault for sharing the information with others (there is that ever so small argument of not talking about others when they are not present, but for the sake of this argument, we are going to ignore that particular social nicety which some people adhere to). In comparison, if you had explicitly told that friend that the information was top-secret level of confidentiality, including within the friend group, and that friend then goes around and shares the information with everyone anyway—they have clearly crossed a very specific and particular boundary. Which, in the second instance, would make any anger or frustration you feel towards that person one hundred percent valid.

See the difference? In the second scenario, you transparently laid out the boundaries that came with the information you had to share; and the friend deliberately ignored them. Whereas in the first instance, you were not explicit in the boundaries of the information, and therefore while it created a mess, the friend who spilled the beans is not entirely at fault.

This type of communication is exactly what is meant when it comes to the personal responsibility of having and communicating your own boundaries. Now, does that mean that you should go up to a store clerk and say "I expect to be treated with respect," without the clerk having done anything to warrant that comment? No, it does not. Thankfully, the majority of us live in societies where common courtesy is still expected and enforced, which makes it easier for you to withhold over-sharing your boundaries to every person you meet. More specific examples of what these 'others' could mean will be covered in later chapters, but for the introduction it was important to begin setting the stage for the responsibility you have of communicating your boundaries.

Your Boundaries and Others

On the other hand, just because you are strong in your boundaries and ensuring they are respected, does not give you the right to trample other peoples' boundaries in the process. Enacting your boundaries is going to be a fine dance of communication, understanding, and respect between yourself and those around you.

For instance, let's say that a friend called Molly and her parents have some pretty strict boundaries about phones at the table during dinner. While Molly respects that boundary she has now taken a remote job where there is a bit of a time difference, Molly is three hours ahead of the company. While the company is okay with Molly not being in the same time-zone, they do ask that she is available to be alerted for work questions or problems during their working hours. Molly agreed to those terms, and made sure that the company understood that while she would respond to a message, she might not get to it right away all the time. Again, the company understood.

So far, so good. Both Molly and the company have

established great lines of communication, understanding, and work boundaries on Molly's availability and the problems of time-change in relation to work projects.

The problem comes up on the weekly Wednesday night dinners Molly and her parents had pre-arranged. Previously, Molly respected her parents' boundary of no phones at the table. However, this particular week, Molly's parents asked that the dinner be moved earlier in the day. When Molly told her parents that earlier was fine, but that she would have to be available for work, her parents agreed.

Fast forward to the dinner and Molly is in the middle of telling her parents that while her phone is on silent, it will have to sit face-up on the dinner table so that she can be alerted if there is a work notification; since that was part of the deal with working for a long-distance company. Molly's parents were not as understanding. In fact, her father insisted she turn it off until dinner was over, which would be about an hour and a half, since the family tended to have longer dinners. Molly told her father that that would not work, because the company expected a reply relatively promptly, since it was their afternoon. Molly even suggested turning her phone on vibrate and placing it on the granite countertop in the kitchen (so that she could hear the vibrations) and answer it in another room. Even to this solution, Molly's parents were displeased, and to please them, Molly ended up messaging her boss and turning her phone off.

Now, to some, that may have seemed like a healthy situation, as many people are now not as fond of having phones at the dinner table if at all possible. The problem is the inflexibility Molly's parents had to the scenario, considering it was her job and not a plethora of social texts or calls.

Molly had a boundary, which she was willing to be flexible on, to accommodate both her job and her parents. Her company was being beyond flexible in Molly's needs. The problem was that Molly's parents were completely inflexible towards the scenario. While it is all well and good to have your own boundaries (and certainly as parents, the ability and need to have more veto-power is definitely necessary up until a certain age), Molly's parents enacted their own boundaries at the sake of their daughters, and even, her employers. While it is completely fair for Molly's parents to have that rule within their own home, and it was completely within Molly's right to find ways to circumvent the problem and attempt to find a solution; Molly's parents were also creating an impossible situation by not being flexible, when they were the ones who created the inflexible scenario by changing the dinner to be earlier and enforcing their rule.

Now, on the flip side, Molly also did something wrong. She turned off her phone and did what her parents wanted to please them. As will be discussed in a later chapter, wanting to please your parents is fine, but if it is at the cost of your own boundary—or even a boundary that may supersede family at certain times, like work—then there is an unhealthy atmosphere and a definite problem.

Workplace and family boundaries will specifically be discussed in a later chapter but it is imperative to understand : Your boundaries are your own and no one else's. That means they should be respected at all times, but that you should not enforce your own at the sake of others.

No Boundaries

Having a hopefully pretty good understanding of what healthy boundaries—and yours in particular—are beginning to look like, it is time to discuss what having no boundaries looks like.

Remember

If anytime during this section you notice uncomfortable similarities, do not be ashamed or worry. We will work through all of this together, and you are becoming more aware. Write down any similarities you notice, and together in a later chapter, we will tackle how to fix it (you may already be getting a basic idea on how to do that now anyways).

Essentially, having no boundaries looks like someone who constantly refuses to acknowledge that they might be the problem. Sounds a bit harsh, right? There are definitely times when it is completely not your fault or problem that something has gone wrong; and this is in no way, an accusation of you saying you should take on the responsibility of something that is not yours.

However, if you are constantly complaining that you feel like people are taking advantage of you, or are overstepping your personal boundaries constantly, it is time to take an honest look at your situation. Yes, there are definitely toxic environments where your boundaries would not be acknowledged or respected, but that is not what this section is discussing.

Often, people with no boundaries are highly aware of what boundaries are, they are just unwilling to acknowledge that part of having boundaries is accepting their personal responsibility to communicate and uphold them regularly. And on the one hand, that is totally relatable because doing so is a lot of work. The problem is that by shirking that responsibility, you are actually creating uncomfortable environments for the people you lash out at when they unknowingly step on your boundaries. Which, to be honest (and you can probably see where this is going), is going to lead to a big old mess with personal relationships. Boundaries are part of what makes personal relationships go round; because it helps people intrinsically understand how to interact around you. Not having any or—better yet—not defining them to yourself and others, is going to ensure eternal conflict.

Having no boundaries that are explicitly stated, or even subconsciously enforced by your words or actions, really does the exact opposite of what you want. Since no one understands what you want or what your own responsibilities are, they will trample all over you while trying to make you and everyone else happy. Which will not only annoy and upset you, but will also create a very messy interpersonal environment for everyone who interacts with you.

Consider this example: You and a friend decide to meet up and get some type of dessert. You mention wanting to get ice cream, and they neither confirm nor deny that that is what they want. So, you pick them up and take them to the ice cream store. Only, once you arrive, your friend gets upset and mentions that the entire time, they wanted to get cake.

While this example sounds a little ridiculous, it was your friend's duty to chime in with their own opinions and wants, and that by not doing so, they deliberately ignored their own wants and boundaries. However, asking them what they might have wanted rather than just assuming could have helped, as well. Yes, calling getting cake instead of ice cream a boundary seems ridiculous, but remember the chapter so far? Your boundaries are what you are responsible for or not, including what you want or not. Therefore, if your friend wanted cake, it was their responsibility to mention this want to you when you asked what they wanted to get to eat. Them not speaking up is first of all, not your fault, and second, their own problem and lack of boundaries.

Small Note

Before going any further it is important to recognize one key difference for any type of boundary, whether it be personal, familial, or professional. If you are in a toxic environment of any sort, no matter how hard you try to enforce or even state your boundaries, they will not be acknowledged on any level.

There is a huge difference between attempting to establish your boundaries with those around you, and having them willfully ignored—between not establishing anything yet still being upset. In the above example, your friend never told you her boundary and want, and as such, the situation became miserable.

On the flip side, if you attempt to state your boundaries to those around you, and no one acknowledges it, and you—understandably—become frustrated; that is a completely different kettle of fish.

Not having boundaries is very, very different from having your boundaries ignored. And that distinction is something that you will have to sit and think about at the end of this chapter (do not worry, there is a journal prompt to remind you).

Journaling

As mentioned in the Introduction, this is the time where some hard-thought truths should be discussed, and a lot of them have been indicated in this chapter so far. To sum it up, take a few moments to sit and think about what has been discussed, as well as a few other probing questions, to get the ball rolling on your own personal boundary journey.

First, begin to write down what you think your personal boundaries might be. Really consider every area of your life and what the big 'no's are in each scenario.

Second, take a look at your communication and understanding so far. Are you willing and ready to communicate your boundaries to those that need to know? If not, take a few minutes and think about why. Is it because you are afraid they will lash out at you? Or that you will get a negative reputation by standing up for your boundaries? If so, finish the journal prompts and continue onto the next chapter (really, you should read the rest anyway, but that was just a great segue).

Third, look at instances where you have felt like your boundaries were ignored. Ask yourself, did you properly communicate your boundary? Did you remind that person in that scenario of your boundary? If you did, journal down your thoughts and feelings along with the specific way that that person ignored your boundaries. Identifying their habits and ticks when they ignore boundaries will help you confront them about it later.

If you were not honest in communicating your boundaries, begin to think of ways that you could for when the next situation pops up. Also, and this one might hurt: be prepared to apologize if you did, and recognize that you acted disproportionately to the scenario because no one was aware of your boundaries; while they did cross your boundary line, it is really hard for them to be careful of something they are not aware of.

Chapter 2

Boundary Myths

Now that you have an idea of what boundaries look like, it is time to discuss what they are *not*, particularly the myths or misunderstandings surrounding boundaries. Please note, that while the word 'myth' is being used here, it is being used to note the false and very far-reaching lack of connection between what the myths are, and how boundaries work.

Unfortunately, boundaries have gotten a bit of a bad reputation, and this is predominantly due to people either reacting poorly to having someone else's boundaries being upheld, or the result of badly used boundaries, such as not being consistent or using boundaries as an excuse for something else.

This chapter will look at boundary myths in two ways: First, we will explain what the myths are, how they work, and possible answers as to why these myths might be in your own life. Second, this chapter will then deal with myth reconsiderations, or ways to re-think these negatives, so that your boundaries going forward will not be hindered by this type of negativity.

While reading through this chapter you may begin to notice some uncomfortable similarities to your own behaviors, habits, or beliefs. And while it will be a bit awkward, embrace those feelings and write them down. Noting where you see similarities between yourself and the following myths are going to be a key component to helping you begin to enact healthier boundaries in your life and relationships. While noting these similarities will be difficult, do not be too hard on yourself. Sadly these myths are perpetuated through misunderstanding and well-guided harmful mindsets. It is your job to think about how the myths are entrenched in your life, why they might be, and how you can confront those behaviors and mindsets going forward in your journey.

Boundary Myths and Reconsiderations

Alright, so, first of all, let's discuss how these myths, or bad mindsets, even came into being. How does something so 'simple' and 'easy' as boundaries get so messed up? Well, unfortunately, that answer is simple: because boundaries are so personal. While they may be easy in some cases to identify (and definitely become easy the more accustomed we are to being attuned to ourselves, wants, desires and responsibilities), this inner understanding and attunement is often where we begin to let the boundary myths come into play. This is done specifically, through the blurring between the lines of what we may believe are our responsibilities, or inner gut feelings of what a boundary is, versus the actuality of what our boundaries are. What makes these misunderstandings even worse is our lack of communication around these boundaries and the insistence on them being constantly honored.

You can spend as much time as you want on defining and understanding your boundaries—which you really should—but if you are unwilling to put the same amount of effort into communicating them and being firm on why your boundaries are what they are, then you will still allow little cracks in your mind for boundary myths to seep in. Particularly when enacting or explaining them.

But what if you are uncertain of your boundaries? For many of us, some of our most intrinsic core beliefs and boundaries are so fundamentally ingrained that we are unaware they even exist, which then makes properly communicating or explaining them not only confusing to ourselves, but also to those around us. Which is why communication is key to healthy boundaries. Nonetheless, good and clear communication is something that many people avoid, do not use, or are unsure of how to use and thus, bad boundaries are created, which in turn perpetuates the problem of boundary myths.

When it comes to our own lives and relationships the myths which will be discussed in this chapter are often enacted through our own misconceptions of how boundaries are portrayed, or are shown through someone we are in relationship with, because they have seen poor boundaries enacted.

Now, if you are someone who has let these myths perpetuate how you enact boundaries, do not worry, and do not let guilt or any type of negative emotion eat away at you. Awareness and open communication will lead the way, and throughout the rest of this book, we will delve into these myths and how to confront them in your thoughts and actions. On the other hand, if you know someone who has experienced these myths and are then projecting the end result of that onto you, make use of your connection to them and discuss it openly and nonjudgmentally. Talking through your boundaries and helping them understand how they will work with you will do marvels in helping to ease another person's fears.

But also remember: There are always going to be times when someone is terrified and/or attempts to resist your implementation of boundaries onto their relationship with you.

Yes, it sucks. Big time.

In a perfect world, we would all respect each other's boundaries and this book would not even be needed.

However, we are human, and sadly that is not yet the case. Therefore, while enacting and enforcing your own boundaries is commendable and highly encouraged, it also comes with the possibility of creating poor reactions in some people. If you remember the Introduction and previous chapter, this is where the personal responsibility and honestly, overall goal of your boundaries, comes in. Having and enforcing your boundaries are mainly for yourself, with the happy side-effect of being healthy for those around you. But it is not the other way around. Do not forget this when going forward with the rest of the chapters, and specifically, when looking and confronting these boundary myths.

Small Note

Before going into the myths, there are two things you should note. First, for this chapter, what you need to begin to understand is that confronting these myths will help you in practicing your boundaries; not necessarily in helping other people understand, respect, or even acknowledge that your boundaries exist. Second, to properly use this chapter, read through the definitions of each myth, the examples, and then the ways that the reconsiderations work in each of the examples.

If any of these things relate to you, take a moment—even grab a highlighter or adjust your ebook reader to make notes, if you have to—to really sit down and analyze those particular examples, what resonates with you, and how it can be battled in your own life.

So, without further ado, let's begin!

Selfishness & Guilt

In all honesty, selfishness and guilt are both the easiest and most complicated forms of boundary myths for several reasons. First, selfishness and guilt play into each other, as both of the emotions—and the triggers of those emotions—tend to coincide. Second, these are two of the most common socially enforced backlashes from when people attempt to begin implementing healthy boundaries in their relationships. Third, both guilt and selfishness have this fine line of being a valid accusation towards you when you enact your boundaries, versus the social enforcement of those feelings for even implementing boundaries.

If that sounded a little too confusing, do not worry, just keep reading. It will all make sense soon, promise.

The Myth of Selfishness

A popular concept that stops many people from wanting to begin implementing boundaries is that doing so would make them seem selfish. Sadly, the birth of this myth could come from anywhere, and to make matters worse, there is a bit of truth to this statement. With the myth of selfishness, there is this uncomfortable reality that, at times, implementing your boundaries will be selfish.

The general understanding of selfishness is that you are either thinking or performing actions without a care for the consequences it could have on others. You are only concerned about yourself and what you need or want. And on the one hand, boundaries should never really get to the extreme of that point—which is where you use your boundaries at the cost or detriment of another person. But… What if it does?

There are definitely going to be times when your boundaries could come at the cost of another human; the difference is that these moments should be extenuating circumstances, rather than daily occurrences. For instance, take the extreme example of you being a witness in a trial for a crime. Your innermost boundary (hopefully) is to be honest with what you saw, even if that incriminates someone who did wrong. Situations like this are not a bad time to be selfish with your boundaries. In fact, many would argue that that is not even being selfish, you are being a law abiding citizen.

So then, why do people view boundaries as selfish? Let's look at it another way: boundaries are a tricky thing, because they are intrinsically built to ensure your own mental health and safety; and it merely benefits those around you, because you are choosing to be a safer and better person. You cannot help others when you are too tired, emotionally drained, or unable to help because you lack the boundaries to take a step back and care for yourself. The problem is, this entire concept of saying 'no' becomes that really messy area where some people's perspectives view that 'no' is selfish. And honestly, it can be. But if used and said properly, 'no' should not be seen in a negative or bad way.

Saying 'no' is something we learn early on in childhood, because we know that the word will stop an action we do not want, need, or like. Why has this become a problem in our adult lives? Because in modern society we have let politeness dictate that we are often unable to say 'no', which is a shame and not incredibly healthy, because it is causing us to forget that 'no' is a basic boundary we need to enact. Now, there is a difference between saying 'no' because it is a specific boundary or you need that particular time, compared to always saying 'no', which will be covered later on in this chapter.

However, if you are saying 'no' to seemingly harmless things like coffee with a friend occasionally, then you are not being selfish by enacting your own boundaries. You cannot help anyone before you help yourself. Therefore, putting yourself last will help no one. If your 'no' is met with "you are being selfish" there is a good chance that the person who said that is not honoring your boundaries, and to watch them carefully. Take a look at the following example:

Over the past few years, you have been noticing that your social battery has been going down. You are more tired than before, and planning events for your different activities has become more of a chore than an enjoyable past-time. On the advice of a friend, you begin to keep a journal of your feelings for each event over a period of several months. During that time, you notice that the main drain on your time, social energy and overall life, is a club where you are the main organizer and chief volunteer. However, this is your longest and most dearest volunteer position, so you begin to become more vocal for several events on how you need the other volunteers' help, with little success. Even implementing their mandatory attendance has done little to help ease all of the work that you end up doing. So, you decide that to combat the social burnout, you are going to step down from being the chief organizer and doer of everything. While the decision is hard, you recognize that this is the only way to ensure that the rest of your social life does not suffer. However, when you tell your fellow volunteers your plan and 'exit' (you are not fully leaving, you are just no longer being the main person they all come to for help), their responses are less than pleasant. Some called you 'selfish' and others asked how the club could possibly run without you. For context, none of those other volunteers had put in nearly half of the time you have over the last year, at the very minimum.

Reconsidering Selfishness

There are several things to note in the above example. First, the decision to step down was not a rash or impulsive decision. It was done with methodical care and deep soul-searching to ensure it was what you wanted and needed. Second, you did attempt to resolve the lack of boundaries with how the other volunteers treated the club and you. While there is the argument that you could have gone farther, let's say that for that argument's sake, in several meetings you did explicitly say "I need more help," and nothing changed. Resigning as the head volunteer was your last resort.

Second, this decision was made to save yourself—therefore, it was a decision based on a personal boundary and the emotional intelligence of understanding what you needed to do to maintain the rest of your life. If you ever notice that something in your life becomes all-encompassing, when that is never what it should be, there is absolutely nothing wrong with taking a step back from it (please note that this is referring to activities, jobs, or non-familial based relationships) . While it is cliche, there is a reason that so many people say, "it's your life," because it is. You get to decide where you spend your time, energy, and so on; and if any of those decisions become too much, and you feel that your own mental, emotional, or even physical health are being put on the line for that position, then something is wrong.

Third, consider how people reacted to your stepping down. For enacting the final thing you can do to save your own mental health and overall well-being, you are essentially being called selfish. Yet, remember, that none of these people had not stepped up to the plate when you repeatedly asked for more help in the past few months. You explicitly stated that you needed help. You gave the others a chance to step up and help you. Now, they will have to pay the consequences for not honoring your boundary or listening to your needs.

In this example, stepping down does not hurt anyone, does not put anyone else's boundaries or health at risk, and it is certainly not jeopardizing a common goal that the group has been striving for. In the example you are not not being a team player; you are putting a stop to being a one-man team.

If, however, you are still unsure, here are a few sure-fire ways your boundaries are being selfish—in a bad way.

First, is when your boundaries cause you to never be available to others. Yes, you should protect yourself, and you are completely within your right to tell someone that you do not have the emotional availability—in that particular moment—to help them. But if you are doing that all the time, then you are using boundaries to avoid being a good friend or family member, because unless there is something deeply wrong (where you should really seek professional help), there should be a time when you are able to help someone else. If you are still unsure, think about group projects, or work. Is there one team member who uses boundaries as an excuse to never really participate in the team? They never stay late, they never socialize, and they never help more than the bare minimum? Yes, having boundaries about the work/life balance are important—do not misunderstand that particular point. It is how that person uses boundaries to ensure that they are never part of the culture, and to not work hard, that is the problem (Mort, 2021).

Second, is when you are using your boundaries to control other people (this does not count if you are the parents of young children, or specific instances which will be covered in a later chapter). What this means is when you use your boundary to ensure that someone else does not have their personal freedom. Consider the difference between these two statements: "Due to my religious preferences, I do not eat pork," versus, "Since I do not eat pork, you should not serve or eat it in my presence either," (Mort, 2021). In the first one, the person is politely stating what they will not eat, but are allowing everyone else in the setting to do as they wish. In the second, the person is blatantly expecting everyone else to bow down to their own boundary while at that event.

Notice the subtle difference?

Small Note

Your boundaries should never be formed to hurt another human. If you are beginning to think that someone else's 'boundaries' are hurting you, find a safe person or therapist to talk that over. Keep a journal of instances where those boundaries are used and your feelings about them, to begin keeping record. Make sure they do not have access to that journal.

The Myth of Guilt

Guilt is probably one of the biggest and perhaps the worst of all the myths surrounding boundaries, because it is one of the most subtle forms of emotions we encounter. There are quite a few times, even in adulthood, where many of us feel guilty over something and we either cannot quite name what it is, or we are unsure if that guilt is even justified. Additionally, many people—maybe even you—are pre-programmed to feel guilty when instigating healthy boundaries; and this could be for a plethora of reasons. Perhaps it is because you feel guilty for putting that type of expectation on a loved one. Perhaps it is because you feel guilty for being selfish. Guilt has this very bad habit of tacking itself onto almost everything and anything, and what is worse, it allows bad behaviors to continue because we bow to the shame it induces.

Have you ever felt the shame of guilt? It is not pretty, and even if that shame and guilt are undeserved, it is incredibly hard to fight. Now add all of those complex emotions on top of instigating boundaries, and it is no wonder that this is a key way many people are able to get in the way of others' establishing their own boundaries, or why some people have a hard time coming up with their own boundaries.

Remember

You should never feel guilty for implementing and standing firm to your own boundaries. Your boundaries are essentially your way of saying what you are willing to be responsible for or not. Ergo, there has been some type of thought (even if it is subconscious) about what you can or cannot handle. Therefore, if you cannot handle something in that particular moment, unless there are extenuating circumstances (which will be covered in the next chapter), you are not at fault for putting your mental and physical health first by enacting your own boundaries.

Going back to understanding how guilt works with your boundaries, or, more specifically, how it ruins your boundaries, let's discuss what happens when someone or something is done to make you feel guilty for defending or using your boundaries.

For instance, Margaret had never really enforced her own boundaries with friends before, but after plucking up some courage, she decided to start. This began with her friend, Tom, who would often well-meaningly buy Margaret a cup of coffee. Margaret would always feel this subconscious pressure to buy Tom a coffee or something else, in return. After thinking it over, and looking at life circumstances which had changed her finances, Margaret began to realize that this was her own lack of boundaries and communication; so the next time she got together with Tom, she asked him to not buy her a cup of coffee, as she could not afford to buy him a treat or pay him back. In response, Tom showed up at

Margaret's with his own coffee and nothing else. While on their outing, Tom asked Margaret if buying the coffee had made her uncomfortable, and Margaret told him about her financial difficulties and how she could not afford to reciprocate Tom's generosity. Tom responded with an, "Oh, I did not know you felt that way when I brought you coffee, I am sorry, that was not my intention." By saying this, Tom was able to signal to Margaret that her feelings of needing to reciprocate Tom's generosity were completely her own and in no way actually projected onto her by Tom.

Now, compare that example to the following:

Compared to Tom, Margaret was also beginning to stand up to her sister Julie. Julie always had this knack of trying to one-up her presents. If Margaret got Julie earrings, Julie got Margaret a necklace, and the escalation would continue. However, for the time being, those types of gifts were no longer something Margaret could afford; and Julie was aware of that. So, when Julie's birthday rolled around, Margaret got Julie a beautiful—but simple—bracelet. It was very pretty and dainty, but definitely not the one-up style that the sisters had become known for. While Julie was thankful for the gift, Margaret could tell that Julie was not as excited about this one, as when Margaret had received a watch for her own birthday. Feeling guilty about the disparity, Margaret bought a sweater—which she could not really afford—for Julie the following day, which her sister received very, very happily.

Reconsidering Guilt

Notice the difference between the two examples. In the first, Tom quickly made Margaret realize that her guilt was unnecessary, and that his gifts and time were not something Margaret had to feel guilty, or obligated, to return. In comparison, Margaret's sister Julie did not do the same. In fact, she subtly encouraged Margaret's guilt over gifts—which could have been subconscious—resulting in Margaret bowing down to her guilt and getting Julie something she could not afford.

Now, there are two things to learn from this example.

First: All relationships do have this subconscious give-and-take mentality. If you are constantly putting way more effort into any relationship than the other person, then there is an imbalance of priorities and you need to address that. It could either be you stepping back, or talking with that friend. On the other hand, this give-and-take is natural and normal in relationships, and is honestly something that should stay in place. This section is definitely not telling you to follow Margaret's example with Tom and to take his gifts and give nothing in return. There is a time and place for everything, and as you will note, in this example it was specifically mentioned that Margaret could not afford it at that time. This is a temporary boundary Margaret has in place to protect herself, and Tom is aware of that and respects it. However, that is not to say that you should begin to enforce a tit for tat mentality. Simply pay attention and ensure that you are not feeling like you are being taken advantage of (or make sure you are not the one taking advantage of the other person) when it comes to time, gifts, or money in relationships, while also understanding the dynamic of that relationship (e.g., do not hold your parents or relatives to the same standard as friends, etc.).

Second: Both of these examples involved money, because money is something that most people feel guilty about intrinsically when there is an imbalance. However, this could be anything, like time spent, or even how emotionally attentive the other person is in comparison to you.

The biggest takeaway you can get when it comes to guilt and boundaries is to look at the intention of the person behind them, and how that person reacts when you subtly shift, or enforce, your own boundaries. Gifts, which include time, items, and emotions, should be given freely, and if they are not, there is a good indicator that the feelings of obligation you have towards that relationship, are a lack of boundaries (Cloud & John Sims Townsend, 2002).

Again, this statement does not involve the natural give and take of a relationship, but it is a clue to beginning to consider your emotions in relationships. If you feel guilty or beholden to certain relationships because they did something for you, you need to sit down and think about why you feel this guilt, and what would happen if you alleviated it by not doing that action, or shifting that action to fit your boundaries better. If the other person is upset by this shift, then there is a lack of boundary understanding you need to address. However, if they go with the flow and do not get upset by that shift, and honor it, then the guilt was an innermost projection.

When it comes to reconsidering guilt, there are two obstacles that have to be faced. First, there is a personal element to the emotion of guilt, because at some point or another, it is something that you not only feel, but may in fact, place onto yourself as well. Good news is that this is one of the easiest to combat on a daily basis. Notice that the phrase says 'easy' not 'enjoyable' or any synonym with that intention. Guilt is easy to combat because there are hundreds of mantras out there to help you fight it on a daily basis. You could make it a screensaver, find an audio/podcast reminder, even set some type of message alert on your phone to go off 'x' amount of times a day, to remind you that you do not need to feel guilty for being healthy with your personal boundaries and to improve your life. On top of that, the majority of the modern world is interested in fighting the guilt many feel when creating healthy boundaries. So not only are there quite a few tools to help you, but the majority of people are actually on your side of helping you combat it as well.

The second thing to reconsider with guilt is that you will be combating more than just a person's own beliefs. Many guilt-based myths surrounding boundaries come from cultural, generational, and personal beliefs surrounding boundaries. Which means that you have to be in top-form to continuously fight it, as well as have a clear understanding of where the implication of guilt is coming from. Or, in other words, why is someone trying to make you feel guilty over your boundaries?

Remember the examples: Julie's enforced guilt onto Margaret was because she was accustomed to getting certain types of gifts from her sister, and was unwilling to accept the financial changes in Margaret's life and the hindrance it would put on her expectations. In comparison, Tom had no guilt put onto Margaret for the change in their routine.

When it comes to Julie, the guilt she subtly enforced onto her sister was based simply out of historical familial expectations—which is something many of us have probably experienced. These are sometimes the hardest forms of guilt-inducing actions to fight, because many people love their family and traditions dearly. In these scenarios, you will need to just grit your teeth and ride out the guilt by saying a mantra continuously in your head. There is really no other easy fix for it.

Selfishness and Guilt Roundup

This particular section has a lot of information pertaining to guilt and shame, which is why it is so long and there are so many sub-categories. Just in case you have any lingering doubts or confusion, here is a brief summation of this segment.

First, selfishness and guilt are more commonly attached to boundaries than we like to think.

Second, you are never selfish, nor should you feel guilty, for enacting healthy boundaries in unhealthy scenarios. If you are putting others before yourself continuously, there will be a time when you are no longer going to be helpful to anyone, and that is not the result anyone wants. There may be times when you are genuinely being selfish by putting yourself first and not saying yes to everything everyone asks of you. And that is okay.

Third, both selfishness and guilt do have the small

potential of being valid accusations if you are enacting or using your boundaries improperly towards others, or badly in situations. For instance, if you are using boundaries to avoid doing something, which could end up being harmful or put more work onto other people who also have strong boundaries, then there is a problem.

Fourth, guilt is toxic and somehow attaches itself to everything that is healthy, mainly because it can come from a variety of relatively understandable reasons. That does not mean that you should let any projected guilt influence how you enact your boundaries. Thankfully, there are many options on how to fight guilt, so you are not lacking help or resources to begin picking and choosing what will work for you.

Myth: Some Relationships Do Not Need Them

Another myth with boundaries is the concept that some people believe they are exempt from your boundaries. To be honest, there may very well be times when these people are, but not for the reasons they think. Those situations are very rare and are for short periods of time, like with newborn babies. It is pretty impossible—and actually really dangerous—to tell a newborn that you have to put yourself first before you feed or change them, without a backup helper in place. If you have someone to help you, then go for it (and honestly, all new mothers should have some type of help for moments like this), but if that help is not there, taking that time and leaving a newborn unattended when they need attention (e.g., they are crying for something) is not the best of ideas. Extenuating, or life phase circumstances, such as: emergencies, newborns, elderly, or those with memory retention problems or special needs, are really the only times that someone should not have boundaries put on them. Mostly because these scenarios encompass situations where your boundaries, while important, cannot simply be enacted at the drop of a hat. You need more preparation and help to do them, simply because these situations are where someone else is depending on you entirely.

Or, on the other hand, there are some people in your life where certain boundaries may never actually affect them, so they may be unaware of that particular boundary. For instance, it is pretty rare for a family member to know a specific, non-generic boundary you have in dating (such as your personal boundaries on physical touch), unless you have discussed your romantic life in detail.

But what about those people who tell you that your relationship with them does not need boundaries?

In all honesty, that is a massive problem, and something that needs to be addressed immediately in your relationship with them. Thankfully, most people are terrified of boundaries due to the lack of communication that often surrounds them, so if you are able to sit down with the person and discuss why they think they are exempt from your boundaries, you may be able to resolve the problem. Or, you may now know exactly why they think they are exempt and decide what to do from there.

A great example would be between Anthony and his cousin Mark. The two had grown up together and were very close, almost like brothers. However, as they began to get older, things got... interesting. The biggest problem Anthony was beginning to face was Mark's newfound belief that his knowledge was the only knowledge that was good, therefore many of Anthony's opinions were ignored or called ignorant or stupid. While Anthony was willing to admit that some of his opinions were a little half-done and were not all well researched or set in stone, they were only teenagers, and there was definitely time for him to learn and sort them out. So, having had enough, Anthony decided to confront Mark. The problem is that the confrontation did not go well. In response to Anthony mentioning that he did not feel like he was being respected, which is a generic and rudimentary boundary, Mark laughed it off and said to Anthony: "Well, it is a good thing we are family, right? Guess that does not really apply to me!"

While on the one hand Mark has a tiny point, as most family members have a special relationship with boundaries (which will be covered in the next chapter), he has got one thing absolutely wrong. Just because someone is family does not mean that they are exempt from your boundaries, or that they do not have to respect them.

No one is exempt from your boundaries, aside from the specific instances which were mentioned earlier.

On the flip side, there could be the potential that you personally think some relationships are exempt from your boundaries. You are not going to like this, but you are wrong. Oh, so, so, wrong. Every relationship—aside from the above exemptions—needs boundaries. You may not like enacting them. You may not be sure about what they look like. But that relationship needs them.

Reconsidering Relationships

When it comes to reconsidering how this myth might have gotten into your life, it painfully starts with the question of who did you allow to walk over your boundaries, because that person was too important to you to lose? The answers to this could be endless. It could be a close family member who guilt-trips you, it could be your own guilt-enforced belief that you cannot, or should not, be firm with that particular person (notice that theme here? How guilt walked right on over from its above segment into here? See, it is one of the most prevalent anti-boundary things in existence). You know what? That's totally understandable, it is scary to set a boundary with someone who blatantly disrespects them, but is still so important to you. Yes, it does happen, and it very well might have happened to you. However, you need to set boundaries. Every relationship needs them.

Your boundaries are what you can or cannot handle, and that includes those around you. That includes those family members, that childhood best friend, your romantic partner, your boss, or coworkers. The guilt you are feeling over including them in the list of people you need to have boundaries with is either through them, or projected from them by yourself. Either way, you need to confront that guilt, because without boundaries in those relationships, you are not going to have a good, healthy, or thriving relationship.

Myth: Boundaries Push People Away

Some people are truly afraid of you putting boundaries on them, because they noticed that people previously used that as a reason to distance their relationship.

Some people use very legitimate and healthy boundaries

on a person who does not have, want, or understand those types of boundaries, and therefore while the boundaries are respected, the relationship still dwindles. These things happen, whether it is because of enforcing boundaries or not. There are probably quite a few of you reading this who are suddenly remembering that friend they once talked to, that you have not heard from in some time. The problem then, is that sometimes, the statement of enforcing your boundaries to that friend, and then the consequent dwindling of the friendship, brings up this nasty correlation which was completely unintentional. However, depending on how those boundaries were specifically stated and enforced, it makes sense that some people are genuinely afraid that boundaries will mean they would lose you as a friend. If this is what you think is happening, then honestly, talk to that friend. If this is a relationship you want to keep, find ways to work through their fear with them, while they also learn to respect your boundaries.

The person who is going to be denied access to you by your boundaries is throwing a small little tantrum over the change in the relationship, mainly because they are frustrated that their control is taken away.

Maybe you are afraid of enforcing boundaries, because you believe it will push people away. Similar to the types of examples and scenarios discussed above, it is completely reasonable to be afraid that some of your boundaries will scare the ones you are closest to away. But in reality, that should not happen.

Reconsidering Pushing

Reconsidering the framing of the above situations should be relatively easy and brief, so here we go.

For the situation where a friendship naturally dwindled but it appeared like boundaries were the main cause, as mentioned earlier, communication is a good remedy to fix that. Talking it through with a friend, or even talking your fears and boundaries through with that person, will ease a lot of fear, guilt, and lack of desire to continue on your boundary journey. If the person is willing, the two of you could even come up with ways to stop both of your fears together. This could be something like having a code word you could both add to a text message, or being okay with over communication. Thankfully, resolving this first fear is easy, once you get past the awkward first bit of discussing your fears.

We mentioned the situation wherein someone else is throwing a tantrum because they lost control over you, and this can be difficult to address, but you must do so anyway. So, call them out on it. Calling out someone who is intrinsically manipulating you is hard because you are not just confronting the unknown of what could happen to your relationship, you are confronting someone who is used to controlling and manipulating you; which means that the conversation could go sideways and you are back at square one. A great fix for this is to bring a safe, neutral, third party (like one of your safe people) who would be able to see through the manipulator's tactics. You could even use that safe person continuously as a fact checker if you decide to stay in contact with that other relationship. Never underestimate the joy and ease of having safe people in your life.

When people are afraid that your boundaries will push them away, here are a few thoughts to keep you going: First, some people may respect your boundaries and while the relationship will shift, it will still exist. Not everyone who is bad at enforcing their own boundaries will drop those that are good at enforcing their own. There is a chance for the relationship to sort itself out once the natural understanding of the new limits has happened. Second, if the person is like the second example above, then in all honesty, who needs them? The people who used your lack of boundaries to control you are not people you need in your life anyways. Same goes for those who are upset with your boundaries because it inconveniences them.

Your boundaries are for your health, and if someone cannot respect or encourage you on that journey, you do not need them.

Small Note

This does not necessarily include the people who have such a bad understanding of boundaries that they panic when you begin to instate them in your relationship. If someone reacts to your boundaries out of fear, try to talk to them about it one-on-one.

If you think or notice someone is acting differently after you tell them about your boundaries, ask them what is going on. If they are honest with you, chances are, you will be able to work it out.

However, if they use your boundaries as a reason to bring up why they should be the exception, or that your boundary is unnecessary, then stop and leave. Just because you are willing to communicate does not mean you can open the door to manipulation or guilt-tripping. Been there, done that, we are not going back.

Myth: Boundaries Are a Sign of Rudeness

Honestly, it makes sense that some people view setting and enforcing boundaries as a sign of rudeness. Depending on your generational, cultural, or even societal background, certain things that some people view as boundaries were maybe not as optional for them when they were forming a sense of identity and intrinsic boundaries. For instance, if someone is vegetarian, but goes to a cultural home and cannot eat half the food, it creates an awkward situation as most cultures view not eating their food as rude, however, the vegetarian's rudimentary dietary boundary is to not eat meat. In this type of scenario, it is best to forewarn the host of any dietary issues, or find a way to bring it up in conversation before the event.

Now that the exception is out of the way, time to confront the people who view your boundaries as being rude. Aside from cultural, generational, or societal implications like the above example, there is never a time when your boundaries are rude. How you enforce them might be. How you explicitly confront people who ignore them might be. But you setting them will never be.

Reconsidering Rude

If you personally feel like you are being rude when you are setting your boundaries, take a moment to consider why that might be. Is it because of how you worded it? If so, go back over that dialogue in your head and really ask yourself if you were being rude, or if you are projecting guilt onto yourself. If you are projecting, remind yourself that setting boundaries is to ensure that you are creating a safe environment for yourself.

Now, if someone called you rude, it is time to confront the elephant in the room. That person is most likely being a bit of a boundary bully. Chances are, they do not like what that boundary does to them personally, and are trying to guilt trip you into backing down. Do not let them. Stand firm. This is not the time or place to bow down to their wishes.

Another question to ask yourself: Could your behavior be construed as rude because you used nonverbal cues (this will be covered later), like excluding yourself from certain scenarios, or avoiding certain people? If you are doing those things and again, the rudeness is self-projected, then it is time for you to recognize a learning curve with boundaries. There will be times when enacting your boundaries will feel rude because you are excusing yourself from situations where you previously ensured you gutted through it. Leaving, ignoring, or being not entirely present (like being on your phone) in those scenarios is not a bad thing. You are silently, or vocally, enforcing your boundaries. As long as you ensure that you are being respectful, you are good to go.

Now, if you are confronted by someone, it is time to

remind them of your boundaries and how those specific scenarios are encroaching on them. If they react poorly, then you know who will not respect your boundaries going forward.

Always Saying "No"

This section will have many similarities to the selfishness segment, but it is still worth discussing on its own. The word 'no' is something that most of us know and respect since childhood. Yet when it comes to boundaries this word is a bit of a *Goldie Locks* situation. Some people never use it, some people use it too often, and others use it just enough. The problem is figuring out what your personal balance for the use of 'no' actually is. Especially since there is a bit of a tricky discrimination between finding what your boundaries are versus either your lack of boundaries, poor communication, or inconsideration towards others (Virro, 2020).

Before your worst fears get a hold of you, let's walk this

through. Setting boundaries means ensuring that you take time to care for yourself and listen to your body when it is telling you that you need to slow down, take a break, or that certain environments are not healthy for you to be in. Think of them as a meter for what you can or cannot do in that particular scenario/life phase. Therefore, on that premise, saying 'no' is actually not that unhealthy.

Armed with that knowledge, let's go through the three types of boundary 'no's again.

The first scenario is those who never use the word. This is actually a lack of boundaries and is very dangerous, as it can cause fatigue, social exhaustion, burnout, and even cause you to be seen as unreliable towards your commitments. Sounds crazy? Take a moment to think about it. It is very likely that you know someone who takes on way too much for their plate. Perhaps they volunteer at too many events, have too many part-time jobs, or say 'yes' to every social event and then are only at each event for half an hour in order to make it everywhere. The majority of people who never say 'no' tend to fall into the people pleasing category; as they are trying to make everyone happy, but are only making themselves, and everyone else, miserable. Some of you are probably thinking: "That's not true! They are the life of the party!"

While this sounds a bit pessimistic… They are the life of the party… for now. Sooner or later their calendar will catch up to them and then they will begin dropping everything like hot pies without an oven mitt.

So, then, how is this actually breaking personal boundaries? On the surface, it may not seem like it, unless you actually have begun a boundary where you will not take on more than you can do. However, this mindset is dangerous for two reasons. The first is that most people expect you to show up when you commit to it. While your friends may be more annoyed at your constant tardiness or canceling; a job, on the other hand, will not be so forgiving. The second problem is when you look at this scenario a bit more closely. The definition of boundaries throughout this entire book is defined as understanding what is your responsibility or not, which then dovetails rather nicely into the entire balancing act of responsibilities versus freedoms versus expectations.

While that discussion is not going to be done here, it does bring up an interesting point of: If boundaries are essentially understanding what you are and are willing to be responsible for, then taking on too many things and not upholding any end of the bargain for any of the things you said you would, is essentially, not fulfilling that definition.

Small Note

This section is by no means saying that you can begin to be that person who simply drops everything at the last minute because your newfound boundary of saying 'no' must be respected. Just because boundaries involve you recognizing what you can or cannot handle, does not mean that you get to be irresponsible and drop everything last-minute. What this does mean is that you can talk to those above you and mention your struggles and together come up with solutions.

The second scenario is the overuse of the word 'no', which in all honesty, is just as bad as the first. Why? Because you are limiting your life a little too much. If you are saying 'no' often because of valid things like: you do not have time, you do not like those people, you do not like that event, then this is not a boundary issue, it is a social/time of life issue which you can either proactively change this week, or you can hope passes with time. However, there are other people who use the word 'no' all the time, and then are upset that they are either not invited to things, missed out on that event, or are afraid that they will not achieve everything they want to do.

Remember: There is a fine line between saying 'no' to respect your boundaries and your goals, and then using 'no' as an excuse to not get there. Do not let your 'no' be an excuse to not get there.

Reconsidering 'No'

The reconsidering of the word 'no' is the same as the third scenario: those who use it just enough, because it means that you have attained the balance of your boundaries and your wants. So, how do you get here? First of all, we need to stop viewing 'no' as this bad word. It is a great intrinsic sign that something is wrong and you need to change.

For instance, if you are the first example of 'no', or, you never use the word, that is a sign that you need to start using it more! The word will not hurt you, the action will not hurt you, and in fact, it may actually give you a tad more freedom. Now, if you absolutely live life full-on, pedal to the metal because you are afraid of missing out, or not being at that one absolutely crazy event, it is really time to think about your priorities and how you can make it all work.

This may seem counterintuitive for this segment, but it is absolutely possible for you to be able to do everything you want. You can be that healthy person who goes to the gym and still has a thriving social life. You can still be a student and work full time. You can still do all of these things and have a full and healthy family life.

So, how do you do it?

So glad you asked. You do it through boundaries!

If it was at all possible, there would be an insert of an evil kitten right above that line. Because having this full and thriving life is exactly what boundaries and open communication gets you. It enables you to set up the life you want, with very little backlash. Now, before you keep going the way you are now, remember: Boundaries include saying 'no'. It can be said with an absolute guarantee that those social media socialites who have and do it all, take time for themselves, say no to some events, and say no to some outings to ensure that everything gets done.

When used appropriately, 'no' will help you get the life you want, and yes, fight all of the innermost thoughts you are having right now about how that sounds wrong. Why? Because notice that the phrase included 'appropriately'. That does not mean you never use it, that does not mean you use it too much, that means you should use it just enough.

And how do you do that?

By understanding your boundaries and beginning to fight the negative connotations the word has. Instead, begin to reconsider 'no' as "not right now". It is amazing how simply changing the word, but keeping the connotation, makes a lot of the fears surrounding it less scary and all intrusive. Saying "not right now" does not mean you will never, or that you will stop. It simply means that for the time you were asked about, you have other plans.

So then, how do you go about ensuring that you use 'no' just enough, in a realistic way? Well, the first thing is to begin figuring out where you are not saying 'no 'enough. That could be anything from all of your life, to simply just your social outings. Identifying where you are unwilling or do not want to say 'no' will help you figure out why you are not willing to limit that area of your life. Once you know the why, you can then begin to combat it.

For instance, if you are limiting your social life because you are afraid that you will miss out on special events, then you can begin to logistically fight that belief by asking yourself how many of those events were actually memorable? Being realistic with your wants versus the reality of your life will help you begin to really see where your memory or hope is getting ahead of where your boundaries should be.

Now for the second scenario, where your 'no' is because you are afraid to leave your comfort zone. There is a big difference between something you intrinsically know is a physical boundary, such as not going on specific rides or doing certain adrenaline based things, and not allowing yourself to be pushed. Honestly, those boundaries are found by trial and error or a deep understanding of yourself and your limits. But, to say the old adage: How do you know if you do not try?

Now, that is not saying to go and bungee jump if you are not an adrenaline junkie or that was never something you wanted to do. And that is also not a green light to put yourself in dangerous scenarios. What this is saying is that if you are using your 'no' to not get to know new people, to not be social with team members, or to not even attempt new things, then perhaps you are using the word 'no' as a crutch.

To combat this, begin with tiny steps. Say 'yes' to that coffee with a friend or coworker that you have been maybe wanting to go to, but originally said 'no' to. Try that new biking trail with a friend. Book that vacation. It begins with the first small step.

Just remember: Do it safely and do it wisely. Do not suddenly become the 'yes' man and then have to re-learn how to instigate 'no' in a healthy way. Instead, learn to instigate 'yes' in a healthy way. Which is to intrinsically ask yourself why your first reaction is 'no'. Is it because that is your habit? Or because you do not want to?

Small Note

While this chapter is a bit of a back and forth mentality, remember this: Your 'no' is enough. Not wanting to go out with that person simply because you do not want to is enough.

When it comes to boundaries and the words 'no' and 'yes', it is a balancing act, but underneath all that balance needs to be this intrinsic understanding of what you do and do not want. Make sure that both your 'no' and 'yes' align with those wants. This will help you maintain and upkeep your boundaries while going to where you want to go and doing what you have always wanted to.

You can have and do it all, but you need your boundaries to get there.

Journaling

This chapter was a lot to take in, so re-reading it, or parsing over certain things that stuck out at you, or maybe did not make a lot of sense, will be important. This is not a sprint, it is a marathon, and the goal of this marathon is for you to understand and know your boundaries and be comfortable to enforce them in any situation you find yourself in. Part of that is to ensure that you understand these boundary myths and how to fight them in your own life and mind.

That being said, as mentioned previously, take a moment and go over the examples that really resonate with your own life. Write down instances where these myths have happened to you, and then begin to restructure and reconsider how you can handle those going forward.

If you are unsure if something is being done properly, find a safe person—or a licensed therapist—who can help guide you on the nuances of your own particular circumstances.

Chapter 3

How to Be More Assertive

Living a life with healthy boundaries includes knowing and understanding how to be assertive with your boundaries. Except, this is something that so many of us struggle with due to any of the previously mentioned myths about boundaries, personality conflicts with assertion, or even just our own confusion on how to be assertive without being rude.

The first thing that you need to know, before even discussing tactics for boundaries in particular, is that as long as you are respectful and polite in your words, and aware of the surroundings and audience you have, being assertive is never rude. It is being calmly and resiliently assured of what you are saying and not allowing peer pressure or bullying to cow you into changing your mind.

Which is all well and good as a statement, but how do you actually go through with it?

This chapter will deal exclusively with strategies you can implement to be more assertive when setting and enforcing your boundaries. You do not necessarily have to use all of them, but you should be able to find a combination that works for both you and your situations.

Strategies for Assertiveness with Boundaries

Asserting your boundaries seems daunting, but there are actually several incredibly practical and easy ways to go about it. Each of them will be discussed individually with examples on how you can begin being assertive, while polite, about your boundaries.

Communicate Your Boundaries

Aha, bet you thought we were done with discussing communication, but we are not. As has been mentioned multiple times throughout this book so far, communication is key in upholding and respecting your boundaries. Additionally, communication has this handy dandy little trick of ensuring that those you talk to respect your boundaries, while also putting your own mind and emotional intelligence on high alert as to whether you are actually doing what you said you would. But how do you actually communicate them to others? Well, there are two very obvious ways: either verbally or nonverbally.

Verbal Boundaries

Verbal boundaries are pretty clear and simple. They are the "I will" or "I will not" statements. The actual phrasing can change, but the intent is the same.

The problem then, with verbal boundaries, is not that they are being openly communicated, but whether you have done so in a respectful, clear, concise, and correct manner. Sounds a bit odd, right? How can boundaries fall into any of the above categories?

Well, boundaries actually go two ways. For your boundaries to be acknowledged and respected, you need to also respect other people's boundaries. And the foundation of this respect is through open and clear communication. How you communicate your boundaries will be the cornerstone of what you expect from others, and what you will or will not tolerate in how they treat them.

Clearly communicating your boundaries will ensure that no one misunderstands them, while also allowing your boundaries to remain fluid to accommodate and change with you, your life and the events and people around you. This also enables you to allow your boundaries to permeate different areas and relationships of your life. While our communication will vary depending on the circumstance, the actual boundary will often not change. For instance, your boundary of being respected is constant throughout every area of your life, but how you communicate that to your coworkers is probably really different from how you would communicate that to friends and family.

Which then brings up an important aspect of communicating boundaries: being polite versus cushioning our wants and needs. So often when we communicate our boundaries, we believe that we need to cushion them with too much politeness, correct phrasing, and unnecessary words to avoid hurting other people's feelings. Which is odd considering that we are discussing your personal boundaries. You know what? Your boundaries should technically never hurt someone's feelings (and if it does, that is a yellow flag that needs to be addressed). How you communicate and enforce them might, but the intrinsic value of your boundaries never should. So then, why do we talk about them like they would—hurt someone's feelings, that is? Why are we constantly apologizing or feeling like our wants, needs, and intrinsic responsibilities are something we should feel sorry for or be overly polite about?

There is a short clip from a television interview with the actress Elizabeth Olsen, where she says one of the greatest pieces of advice that her family ever gave her was that, "No is a full sentence… you can just say 'no'," (theoffcamerashow, 2021). The simplicity of this statement and belief cannot be denied, especially when it comes to our boundaries. While the actual phrasing of our boundaries might not include the word 'no', there is still some element of that word in the boundary (i.e., "I will not eat pork", "I do not kiss on the first date"). You do not have to soften your 'no's to make them more palatable for other people. In practical terms, what this means is that saying your boundary, without the unnecessary flamboyance or politeness, is enough.

Another crucial element of communicating your boundaries is ensuring that you state them in the appropriate time and place. You can be as polite, or as simplistic as you like when stating your boundaries, but if you do it at the wrong time and place, they will not be acknowledged, respected, or even considered the first go round.

Would you really listen to someone's boundaries at work if they just randomly stated: "I do not like going by that nickname anymore," during a team meeting? Most likely not. In fact, you may not even acknowledge what they said at first.

Communicating your boundaries is not just ensuring that you are simply and clearly stating your intent, or what you are or are not willing to be responsible for. It is also ensuring that you are doing it in an atmosphere of acknowledgement and receiving.

Receiving does not necessarily mean that the listener will honor the boundaries; it merely means that you have somehow ensured that the atmosphere is aware that you are going to speak and they need to noticeably acknowledge that you said something. Yes, that sounds awkward, but remember: People have the ability to not respect or remember your boundaries. Including when you have prepared the room to do so. Some boundaries—especially when it comes to consent, or you feeling or being unsafe—do not need an appropriate time or place.

Nonverbal Boundaries

These boundaries are a bit trickier, as they tend to forego the golden rule of this book which is to actually communicate (speak) your boundaries in a clear, precise manner in the correct context. So, nonverbal boundaries are something that should be used as a last resort, or perhaps as the first tiny step to beginning to communicate your boundaries.

Nonverbal boundaries are simply the act of you leaving, stopping, or not participating in something. Which is part of why they are a gray area of boundaries: They are not clear, precise or necessarily understood, acknowledged or perceived by those around you.

So why would someone use them? Simple: Nonverbal boundaries are the first step for yourself, on how you are going to take a stand for your actual boundaries.

No, this does not mean to create a post-board sign with your boundary written on it and walk around your office, home, or school. However, this could be you leaving the room quietly when you notice that gossip has taken over the conversation. The problem is that this type of action becomes a double-edged sword because while it allows you to begin getting comfortable being different in a crowd and to begin asserting your boundaries without yet vocalizing them, nonverbal boundaries have this precarious characteristic of appearing rude. If your friend suddenly was on their phone the entire time you and your friend group was having a conversation, which you viewed as harmless, would you think that was a boundary, or that they have checked out and no longer want to be there? Most likely the latter. Yet, for all you know, this could be your friend's silent way of signaling that they are uncomfortable.

So, while nonverbal boundaries may be necessary for either very strenuous situations (like tense work meetings), or something you intrinsically need to begin feeling more comfortable asserting yourself, use them sparingly and wisely. And, if need be, address them later on when you are finally able and comfortable to verbalize your boundaries.

Be Proactive

There are so many times in our lives where being proactive could save us a world of hurt, and boundaries are certainly one of them. How to be proactive with setting your boundaries is to start early. Setting boundaries early, as we learned, can require very good communication, but getting ahead of an unnecessary conflict can save you a lot of emotional time and energy (Castrillon, 2019).

A great example of being proactive with your boundaries is by mentioning them at the beginning of a new relationship, or not letting the little things slide. For example, letting the barista at your local coffee shop know that your drink is wrong is a great example. While how your coffee is made may not be an actual boundary, mentioning that your order is wrong, is respecting the boundary of your specific need at that moment.

This might seem a little patronizing, but bear with it for a moment. Part of the reason why you want to practice being proactive with your boundaries in the little things, is not just so that you become more assertive through practice, but also so that you are able to begin enforcing how your boundaries look to yourself.

If you are unaccustomed to setting boundaries, then being assertive—let alone proactive—are going to feel unnatural and almost like you are over-communicating to those around you. While it may be slightly true, for now, take that trait over not respecting or enforcing your boundaries, and simply begin to practice journaling or looking back at conversations in hindsight (at least an hour after you have had them) so that you can analyze if you over-communicated or if you were actually combating a boundary reactive fear or myth.

Practice, Practice, Practice

There is the old adage that "practice makes perfect", and in the case of boundaries, it is true. Being politely assertive is something that comes with practice. Even if you are naturally inclined to be assertive and very open about your wants, needs, and boundaries, practicing this assertiveness politely will never really steer you wrong.

In case you are wondering how you can practice being assertive, sadly, it is truly by just *being* assertive. This might sound too simple—because it is—but the real problem will come with you actually following through with it.

Helping you follow through with practicing your

assertiveness for boundaries is going to be just as simple. Pick one or two small boundaries that consistently get crossed over (e.g., your coffee is not properly made, you let customer service workers be rude to you, or you let people around you be rude to you), and begin standing up for yourself.

Realistically, nothing else is going to help you combat your aversion to assertion, other than actually taking a breath and doing it.

That being said, your discomfort over that idea is completely understood. It is something that many of us deal with, but the only way to get through it, is to do it. Think of it as immersion therapy. It will only get better the more you do it and practice it.

Give Yourself Grace

The definition of 'grace' is the "disposition to or an act or instance of kindness, courtesy, or clemency, or a temporary exemption" (Merriam-Webster, n.d.). When it comes to how to give yourself grace, it means to acknowledge when you tried but failed, or when you failed and to not beat yourself up about it. This is especially true when it comes to being assertive with your boundaries.

There are going to be days where you are not going to be assertive on all of your boundaries, there are going to be days where you just cannot give the emotional energy to stand up or maintain them, and there are going to be days where you are being assertive or communicate your boundaries poorly. And you know what? It is okay.

We are all human, and we are all learning and figuring this out together, one day at a time. None of us are perfect, even though some try to give that impression. We are all going to have incidents, moments, or scenarios where we admit—even to ourselves—that that entire series of events could have gone better. Forgiving yourself, learning from it, and moving on with that knowledge is the key to getting yourself out of self-pity and into receiving your own grace.

Now, that is not a "get out of jail free card" for when you are too lazy, or not feeling like standing up for your boundaries or communicating with them properly.

Because while you may be able to—and should—give yourself grace, the other parties may not be so inclined. And that is something you have to accept and be okay with, because if the tables were turned, would you forgive yourself?

Giving yourself grace is necessary, but not doing the work and then still asking and extending yourself grace—while it may happen on the occasional blue moon—is something you want, and should, avoid.

Do not take advantage of giving yourself grace to avoid doing the hard work; because you will not get farther on this journey and may do yourself more harm than good.

Combating Assertion Guilt

As mentioned before, guilt has this nasty way of attaching itself to almost anything and everything, including you beginning to assert your boundaries. So how do you combat the guilt that can come from your assertiveness?

By remembering the following:

You asserting and standing up for your boundaries, as long as it is done politely, is never something to feel guilty about. You are just as worthy of having your boundaries understood and respected as anyone else. You are just as worthy and capable of standing up for them as anyone else. Your boundaries are something you are able to be firm on, and you know yourself enough to know that your boundaries are worth fighting for.

Combating Your Weaknesses

First of all, let's get something clear: just because a few (or all) of these strategies are daunting does not mean that you cannot do this, or that you are intrinsically weak. It means that you have not had the ability to practice being assertive with your boundaries.

Which we will combat right here and now.

If any of these things are something you struggle with,

take a moment to write them down and begin to ask yourself why they are hard for you. In your answers, do you notice anything to do with the boundary myths that were discussed? If so, you already have a good idea on how to begin rephrasing and combating those fears.

If standing up for yourself is difficult, it could be for many reasons: it could be something you are not confident in, something that has been ingrained into you from your culture, family, or society, you could be a people pleaser, or it could be because you are afraid that you will lose the relationships you assert boundaries in. Let's combat each of those worries individually.

Ingrained Behaviors

Unfortunately, boundaries are something that some of us learn from the cradle, while others are taught that it is a selfish pattern of behavior. If this is you, remember that boundaries are not a selfish behavior, and they are something that will be immensely helpful in your life and relationships going forward. Regrettably, what this also means is that you are going to have a time in re-learning how to think about your behaviors in order to ensure that you are confidently enforcing your boundaries. Good news is that you now have tools to reshape and combat the guilt you have been programmed to feel for sticking to your boundaries.

So, then, when it comes to combating the actual cause of your ingrained behaviors, begin by thinking where it originally came from. Was it a saying that your parents told you? An incident at school? Or how a friend or sibling scolded or even talked to you when you were younger? Identifying the underlying element of why you intrinsically believe that your boundaries are wrong will help you begin to find a strategy to fight them without feeling guilty.

This strategy that you come up with, as with everything in this chapter so far, is going to be relatively easy in theory, but incredibly difficult in practice. You are going to have to fight it with contradicting mantras.

For instance, if you were told as a child that your boundaries were something that you did not need to share, or were unnecessary, a simple way to combat that is to remind yourself that they *are* necessary, you *do* need them, and they *will* help you.

Again, easier said than done.

People Pleasing

Another reason why so many are unwilling to be assertive with their boundaries is because they are people pleasers.

Yes, you read that right.

People pleasing is actually a form of not respecting your own boundaries, because by the very definition, a people pleaser is someone whose emotional need to help others will come at the cost of their own (Merriam-Webster, 2022). Therefore, if you are a people pleaser, you are wired to ignore your own boundaries to please others, if that is what it will take.

Sounds a bit odd?

If your innermost desire or need is to please other people, sooner or later, your boundaries will upset someone—that is a sad fact of life. Which then means that you will be put in the awkward position of choosing between pleasing that person and honoring your boundaries, or discarding whatever boundary you have set to please the other person. While it is hoped that you would find a way to mediate between the two, but ultimately be willing to choose your boundaries over the other person, there is a very low chance of that happening if you have not already practiced foregoing your people pleasing tendencies.

Before closing this section off, two things should be noted. First, people pleasers are not bad people, they just have this bad tendency of foregoing their own needs for others when they really should not. If you are a people pleaser, do not worry, there is a whole chapter devoted to ensuring that you are firm and assertive with your boundaries in your life. Second, fighting people pleasing is hard, and that inner turmoil should never be belittled.

People pleasing is an ingrained habit that is sometimes done out of either a need or trauma, and either way, you are fighting what are most likely years-long habits in order to begin changing. That task is daunting, but you do not have to do it alone. That being said, if you are a people pleaser, or someone who has people pleasing tendencies, setting boundaries is going to be tricky for you, especially when it comes to boundaries and interpersonal relationships. Which means that you are going to have to work a bit harder than some others on your boundary journey.

A Few Tips

There is absolutely no way that you are going to be left hanging on what to do if you identify or are a people pleaser. In this segment a few things will be quickly mentioned to help you gain some perspective before discussing interpersonal relationships. Use this section wisely: Get your journal, write a few ideas down, take a few minutes to begin coming up with your own spin on the solutions that are presented here, and begin to enact them once you have a good handle on what to do. Fighting people pleasing will be hard, but in this instance, practice truly will make perfect.

First: Actually communicate your boundaries. It sounds

odd, but communicating your needs and wants will help you begin to see who will respect your boundaries or not. And this is important as it will bring up our second tip (Tartakovsky, 2019).

Second: Only focus on the relationships that will nurture you (which you can identify by the people who will respect and encourage you setting healthy boundaries). As mentioned in the previous chapter, if someone does not respect your boundaries, even when you try to talk it through, then that is someone who is not necessarily going to encourage a healthy relationship with you—or even a healthy version of you. Those types of relationships will aim to take advantage of your people pleasing tendencies, which has a high likelihood of resulting in you being burned out and not getting what you need from that relationship (remember: relationships are all give and take, you cannot always be the giver).

Third: Begin to put yourself first. Often people pleasers put their identity and fulfillment of wants and needs onto/from/in other people. Not only is that dangerous for you as a person, but that is a blatant disrespect of your own boundaries; you are not accepting any responsibility for what you can or cannot handle, and are putting that entirely onto another person. While that may seem odd, since people pleasing tends to mean that you are doing everything possible to please someone else, remember the definition of a people pleaser: Their emotional wants and needs are intrinsically tied to fulfilling someone else's wants or needs (Merriam-Webster, 2022). That means their fulfillment will come from whatever they do to make someone else happy. While it is completely natural, healthy, and encouraged to feel happy when we make someone else happy, putting all of our ability to actually be happy off of someone else's reaction to our actions is not only convoluted and a lot of back and forth for some happiness, but it is also a good way to make someone else resentful of you over time, as well as ensure that you never actually know how to satisfy yourself on your own; neither of which are good or healthy places to be.

Again, if any of these things are you, or if you align with anything in this segment, do not worry or lose heart about your boundary journey. These three things were brought up so that you could begin to recognize and fight them in your life, not so that you could stop and lose heart. You can do it. You can set healthy boundaries and have healthy relationships; and it will actually feel so much better once you do.

Losing Relationships

The fear of losing relationships while asserting your boundaries deeply mirrors the myth of pushing people away, or those who feel that they are exempt from your boundaries—but with a bit of a twist. This twist is that you may be actually afraid of confrontation.

Wondering how we made that switch?

Confrontation is often seen as a companion to asserting your boundaries because so many people attempt to do it wrongly, or are pushed to their breaking point and then explode with their boundary communication. Both of these scenarios then present as a chaotic form of confrontation, which many people have a natural, or ingrained, aversion to. And if that natural aversion occurred when communicating a boundary, it makes sense as to why some people do not necessarily want to assert their boundaries.

If you are afraid to be assertive with your boundaries because you believe that will bring up a confrontation, answer the question of why this would bring up a confrontation. Is it because the other person has responded explosively to boundaries in the past? Is it because your boundary is in direct violation of theirs? Or is it because you are intrinsically standing up for yourself, and they are unaccustomed or do not want that?

How you answer these questions will then dictate how you should respond to the fear of losing that relationship. If it is because the person has exploded reactively in the past, begin to consider why that person exploded. Was it because of poor communication? Because that boundary violated or triggered them? Look at the scenario and begin to think of ways that you can present your boundary differently to avoid that outcome. There is a good likelihood that you may be able to avoid that type of response if you handle the situation properly

Small Note

If this is the type of person who is volatile and will never respond properly to your boundaries, seek professional help, and leave if you have too. Boundaries were meant to help heal, form, and maintain strong and healthy relationships. They were not meant for you to stay for duplicity, addition, or abuse of any kind.

Now, back to the second reaction, did someone react poorly to a boundary assertion because that boundary directly violated theirs? If so, then really consider the situation and why that boundary violated someone else's. Boundaries should never do that, unless someone is a manipulator, liar, or is using boundaries as an excuse to get away with poor behavior. Therefore, technically, healthy boundaries should mostly be in alignment with each other, and as long as you communicate (see how often this pops up?) properly, you should be good to go. However, if while you were analyzing that past scenario, you begin to notice that the other person's boundary is unhealthy—or that yours might be—seek professional help either from a counselor or safe person on how to address that specific person or boundary.

The third and final scenario is if the other person does not want, or is unaccustomed, to you asserting yourself. If someone does not want you to assert yourself, then leave. They will not be a healthy addition to your boundary journey and will definitely not be a safe person to support and guide you. Again, please note: This only applies if your boundaries are healthy and respectful of yourself and others, and if you have tried to assert yourself respectfully in the past.

Now, if someone is unaccustomed to you asserting yourself and has reacted poorly, consider giving them grace and talking about it either on your own, or with a safe person, therapist, or mediator. That reaction may require figuring out how to make sure that your boundaries are heard while they work through their own fears and boundaries. Thankfully, you can both figure out how to combat those together.

Journaling

Now that you know what boundaries are, what

Boundaries look like, and how to be assertive and confident in your boundaries without guilt, it is time to practically take a few moments to think through which strategy will work best for you.

In all honesty, a combination of everything that has been mentioned would be ideal, but some may take longer or more practice than others—and that is okay. Figuring out how you personally are going to be assertive is not an immediate thought or action; it is you testing out different things, confronting certain fears or boundary myths, as well as constantly checking yourself to ensure that you are being assertive without being rude.

So, with that in mind, take a few moments to pick the assertive strategies you naturally excel at, as well as the ones that scare you, or you are not strong at. Begin to make a plan on how to be stronger in all of the assertive strategies. A good way to start is by picking one and attempting it the next time you need to communicate your boundaries.

Do not forget to give yourself grace while practicing.

You may not get it right the first time, and that is okay. You can do this.

Chapter 4

Setting Boundaries in Relationships

Now that we have gone over how to be assertive with your boundaries, it is time to look at each area of your life to see exactly why you need to set boundaries and how you can start. In this chapter we will discuss how to see where these areas of your life do, or do not, have boundaries, and where to go from there.

Extenuating Circumstances

As mentioned previously, there are times where your boundaries are going to encounter extenuating circumstances. These specifically refer to areas where you are not safe, in personal danger, in relationship with an extremely unsafe person (like addicts, serial liars, psychopaths, or sociopaths), or in certain life phases such as with newborns or elderly/dementia patients, where boundaries need extra steps.

If you are in an unsafe relationship or scenario, know this right now: No boundary is going to save you.

Addicts, serial liars, manipulators, psychopaths or sociopaths will never respect your boundaries, and you should not continue to put yourself at risk. Understanding and setting your boundaries will help you going forward once you exit that relationship, but for the immediate future: Get out. Find a safe person who will help you get away to a safe place where you can gain perspective.

If you are in one of those strange life phases where your boundaries will honestly not be a lot of help with one particular relationship (such as a newborn, dementia or specific elderly relatives/people you know), then really the best way through it is to stick up for your boundaries the best way you can (this is specifically for the elderly or dementia patients), but extend a lot of grace to the situation.

Consider this example: Michelle's grandmother has extreme bipolar disorder, as well as heavy depression, which has made her incredibly volatile and emotionally unstable over the years. The family had developed methods to cope, but now the grandmother has developed terminal breast cancer, and the family has been given six months. Michelle, while aware and firm on her boundaries, was one of the main care-givers during this time. While she did not tolerate verbal abuse from her grandmother, she also did not correct every little thing, or pay attention when her grandmother had just taken her heavy pain medication.

While this example is incredibly depressing, it perfectly showcases a time in some people's lives where their boundaries are still important, but there is this awful give and take on when to enforce them, versus when to let things go. In the case of Michelle, this example showcases that as one of her grandmother's main caretakers for the limited end of the grandmother's life, Michelle recognized that her boundaries were important and needed to be honored; but her grandmother also needed help and would not always entirely be herself due to medication and the effects of specific treatment.

Remember the previous chapter on when it was appropriate to enforce your boundaries? Enforcing them to a patient who is incredibly high off of painkillers, or incredibly sick and tired from serious medical treatment, is one of those times.

Small Note

Now, this is not to say that Michelle would let her grandmother verbally abuse her, or let her grandmother's mental conditions get in the way of how her grandmother constantly treated her. However, there is also the fine line of insisting that an unhealthy person (in this case due to the bad mental health of a dying patient) maintain healthy mindsets versus incredibly stressful and depressing circumstances.

The problem with any extenuating circumstances which

have been mentioned is that they are incredibly special and specific to you, your boundaries, and the situation. For instance, some people might be in Michelle's shoes, but need their boundaries to be more respected, even during that time, due to previous traumas of their past. That is completely okay. Because these types of situations are so specific, if you are unsure or not able to monitor yourself and what your boundaries can or cannot handle, use a safe person or therapist who can help guide you. Not because you are unable to do it yourself, but because these scenarios are inherently stressful and having a third, neutral opinion might help you gain a better perspective and figure out what to do.

Now, going back to relatively normal relationships and the boundaries needed in those relationships. This section will be divided into the main elements of your life (family, friends, work, and romantic relationships). Each section will discuss how these boundaries work, and give examples on what communicating/using them may look like.

These examples specifically cover each area (roughly) of your life for several reasons: First, it will help you to really see and debunk any of the previous boundary myths you may think you are unconsciously enacting, but are unsure of. Second, while boundaries are something that encompass and transcend every part of your life, the enactment and firm way to uphold those boundaries may be slightly different depending on who you are with and the situation. Third, once you begin to see how a simple boundary, like "I do not like hugging people", can transcend and morph between the different areas of your life, you will be able to be more consistent when enforcing your boundaries—while simultaneously beginning to ensure that your boundaries are fluid enough to stay firm to what they are, but adapt to different situations and relationships.

Setting Boundaries With Family Members

When it comes to families there is one relationship where boundaries become a bit of a sore spot, and that is with authority figures and parents. While this section will also cover siblings, parental and authority figures will definitely consist of the lion's share for one very important reason: the power dynamic shifts throughout the course of our lives, and so too, will our boundaries and how the respect for those boundaries is enacted.

Parents and Authority Figures

Enacting and consistently enforcing boundaries with parents or authority figures can become a mental minefield of navigating either self-induced, or enforced guilt and feelings of shame and/or selfishness, along with just trying to gain a basic understanding of respect versus overstepping boundaries. And the fluidity of the relationship between parents and children in regards to power dynamics and boundaries does not help the situation.

What this power shift is alluding to is the growth of the children and how boundaries and responsibilities shift as we grow. When we were younger, or minors, the power lay mostly with the adults. Therefore, while boundaries were hopefully still in existence, certain wants and needs, or extensions of boundaries, were not always as debatable. In comparison, as adults, our boundaries should be respected and acknowledged; yet how that actually looks becomes a bit of a foggy mess that can cause confusion, angst, and a lot of miscommunication.

Please Note

The above statement has absolutely nothing to do with fundamental human right-based boundaries such as: physical, sexual, and emotional safety, nourishment, or simple lack of abuse.

If any of those things occurred—or are occurring—get professional help. This could be a therapist, a friend or other authority figure who you trust, or authority figures in your community who will believe and listen to you.

If this happened to you, first of all: That is awful, and you did absolutely nothing to deserve it. Second, your boundaries will come with heavily related traumas, and you should seek professional help (such as a therapist or counselor) when you begin to address and resolve the boundaries that have been broken. While this book will help you, it will not cover traumatic events or triggers specifically (they will only be mentioned), and that type of help should honestly be reserved for professionals.

Changing Boundaries

Now, back to authority figures and boundaries. As previously mentioned, these types of boundaries tend to morph and change when power dynamics shift, or, as we grow. Take body modifications, like tattoos or piercings, for example. As a minor (depending on where you live) there is most likely an age limit on when you can get these things done without the consent of an adult/authority figure who is a predominant guardian. However, as we get older, those types of enforcements no longer exist. Once you come of age, you can get any type of modification you want. The problem (and why this whole section is being written) then becomes the personal boundaries of living situations, parents, you, the power shift of your home, etc. Handling and figuring out how those boundaries work are honestly a tumultuous and incredibly sensitive time, which is why reading and understanding the different phases from both perspectives (children and parents) is going to be addressed.

Because this section is large, it will be parsed into multiple views to discuss the various angles.

First, we will discuss younger boundaries, where you as the reader will be able to gain insight on how certain boundaries may or may not have been respected from your childhood. Then we will move onto older boundaries which will roughly be teenage to young adult years. This section will specifically discuss how certain power shifts will affect your boundaries, and how to deal with that. Each of these sections will then have their own perspective section for parents of that age group.

The goal of parsing these sections up in such a way is to help you gain perspective on your childhood and possibly why your parents may have handled things in a certain way, or, conversely, to see what healthy boundaries when you are a young child or teenager with healthy boundary respecting parents looks like—with the hindsight of being an adult who is now armed with a good foundation of knowledge on boundaries. Additionally, with the added sections of parental perspectives, you will hopefully be able to glean not only an understanding of what parents go through, but be able to see the vast difference between fully formed and functioning adult boundaries versus children's boundaries, and how your own have morphed over time.

Understanding how your boundaries have changed will accomplish two things. First, it will help you begin to realize that even now your boundaries have the ability to be fluid as life changes. Second, it will help you begin to really see how certain boundaries you may have thought were being disrespected by your parents, most probably were not. Or, on the very awful chance that they were, confirm your suspicions.

Younger Boundaries

When we are younger, our parents hold the majority of power over our lives. Honestly, it sounds harsh, but this is most likely for the best (if you are beginning to get annoyed, do not worry, just keep reading). Our parents or authority figures have years of real-life world experience, meaning that they most likely (sadly, not always) are able to use that wisdom to help us grow.

For instance, most parents or authority figures know that you should not wear shorts when it is snowing outside, yet as a three-year-old, that logic may not be understandable or even fully formed. Which is where boundaries come in. Parents have the authority and boundary knowledge to ensure that those who are of primary school age or younger cannot do those types of things, or put themselves into dangerous or harmful situations.

However, that type of authority also comes with heavy responsibility. It is hoped that while the authority figures have this type of power/dominance of their own, that they will be able to teach you responsibility and wise decision making to the point where you will be able to function and continue to grow on your own, once this balance in power begins to shift (the next section).

What this means is that when we are younger, our boundaries should still be respected, but in comparison to older boundaries, younger boundaries are more so taught and felt, than cognitively perceived. Four year olds know perfectly well what they will or will not tolerate or accept, but they may not be completely able to tell you why. Most parents, when you look at them closely, seem to intrinsically (or they have done a lot of book reading on the subject, hopefully) understand which boundary is intrinsic to their child, versus ones that may have to be walked through to either see why their logic is wrong, or to help them better define what their boundary actually is.

So what does this mean for you, a fully grown and mainly functioning adult? Well, sometimes as young children we predominantly feel like our boundaries were wronged, but are unable to fully explain why. And unfortunately, there are some cases where that could be true. If you believe this is you, then it is strongly recommended that you find professional help to begin working through that trauma. However, for most of us that may not be the case. Think back to those moments where you felt severely wronged as a young child, and then begin to look at it through the eyes of your now boundary-knowing brain. Were your boundaries being disrespected, or did your parents or authority figures just not explain their reasoning behind it well?

Consider this example:

Even though it happened decades ago, there is still a small part of you that is upset (even though you understand that you need to let it go, because it was years ago) that your parents seemed to always make you share your toys, but your cousin—to your knowledge—was never made to, either.

Put into adult perspective, most of us are also aware that these types of annoyances are irrational and not relevant anymore. However, that annoyance has a teeny, tiny, kernel of truth/acceptance to it, because it signifies that we were unable to let go of a transgression that happened to us. In this instance, it was that you were made to share, while your equal was not. Therefore, the very boundary of equality and respect—something many of us know from an early age—was, in our minds, deeply wronged. However, as adults, we are able to recognize that we did not know the other side of that story. Perhaps your cousin was forced to share and you do not remember it, or they lied about it. Whatever the reason, understanding why we are still angry over the transgression of boundaries from our childhood years will be fundamental knowledge in understanding how certain frustrations may be playing out now—especially when it comes to enacting and enforcing healthy boundaries with people you may already have a decades long grudge against.

Parents of Younger Boundaries

On the other hand, setting boundaries as a parent can be just as daunting, because now you are responsible for ensuring that this little human is somehow a functioning adult with hopefully relatively healthy boundaries. And, depending on the age, your ability to get the child to understand boundaries is going to be an uphill battle.

Thankfully children's boundaries develop very quickly; and it is the job of the parents to not only honor those boundaries, but help if they are a bit out of alignment. For instance, going back to the shorts and snow example. What if the child was now thirteen, instead of four? Suddenly the parent is faced with a difficult choice of playing the parental card of "you still cannot wear that," versus letting them test those waters to learn the lesson and figure out if that boundary was worth fighting for.

Now, that is a lot of moving factors for one child.

Imagine two or three. Now imagine they are all growing and reaching new milestones roughly every couple months or every year, depending on the age. Hopefully, you are beginning to get the idea of how parents struggle to sometimes understand and recognize every single boundary that is thrown their way.

Again, that is in no way an excuse for parents who deliberately ignore their child's boundaries; and that is certainly not saying that any type of abuse or neglect (physical, emotional, addiction, duplicity, etc.) are okay on any level.

What this does mean is that some of us as adults specifically remember a time when our firm and emphatic 'no' based boundary was not respected, and while that memory may still bring up intense feelings of frustration, hurt, or anger, you may also be getting an inkling as to why that boundary was ignored.

If you are a parent with young children, then here is a great rule of thumb: Teaching them about responsibility, if done right, will never go wrong. The more young children are responsible (as long as it is age appropriate, like cleaning their toys), will help them begin to understand the intrinsic relationship between their boundaries and the responsibilities that go with it.

That does not mean to give your child more than they can handle, or that you should make everything about responsibility. Again, it is all about balance.

Boundaries of Adult Children

Compared to small children, teenagers and adult children (essentially anyone in their twenties and up) possess fully formed and functioning boundaries; and it is at this stage that the power dynamic begins to stir up friction. Remember the teenage years? Or perhaps you are a teenager now. It might very well feel like your parents are not respecting your boundaries. And, sadly, for some of you, they might not be.

However, on the small chance that your parents might be, or did, respect your boundaries, begin to think about the reasons why certain things were denied. For instance, that age-old adage of "not under my roof!", was a pretty common one a couple of years ago. And, while it may be irksome, while it may be annoying, that is a boundary parents and authority figures are more than allowed to have. And ones that should be respected as long as they are reasonable.

Going back a few examples, it is perfectly reasonable (but can one hundred percent totally suck) that your parents have a rule or boundary where you are not allowed to get any new body modifications while living under their roof. Which is also why so many people get them the minute they move out during their university years. Respecting that boundary of your parents is your duty because: they are the adult, it is their house, and for your boundaries to be respected, you have to respect theirs.

And while it is really painful on a certain level to say this: You wanting a body modification (or something like that) is not a boundary violation. However, at the same time, your parents putting restrictive boundaries on you not only causes friction, but can also create many gray areas of how to handle boundaries. For instance, if you are twenty one and your parents are still not allowing body modifications in their home, while it is their right to have that rule in their house, it also becomes awkward because you are twenty one, and that type of boundary is a bit restrictive for your age.

You can always combat that by attempting to have a sit-down communication with your parents, or by moving out. Again, their house, their rules; which is perfectly respectable. Especially since body modifications are not a fundamental human right.

Sounds messy, right?

As an adult child, begin to think about your boundaries and why they are important to you. For instance, using the body modification example, the modification is not the boundary, but having your parents respect your ability to make wise choices might be. Confronting your parents has to be done with respect and awareness of the bigger picture. Simply going up to them and saying, "I am an adult and can do what I want!" will get you nowhere, and will just result in a large fight or make further progress a lot harder.

What Those Boundaries Look Like

Regardless as to your living situation, here are a few

things you can do to begin implementing healthy boundaries with your parents as an adult child.

First: You can assemble the boundaries—and their enactments—you want respected. Take a good long look to see if they deliberately violate any of your parents own boundaries, such as ingrained house rules, or specific responsibilities or values they personally have. If your boundaries violate theirs, or are specifically going against their beliefs, you may have to re-think either your living situation before discussing your boundaries with them, or, ensure that you walk them through your logic to get to a middle ground of mutual understanding and respect.

Second: Be assertive, but compassionate and open to communicating or answering questions they might have. It might sound silly, but you will always be your parents/guardians child, so when you confront them with very adult-like boundaries, they may intrinsically panic. And you may have to be the bigger person and help walk them through what this will look like, and how you will ensure your safety. Being open to communicating and answering questions will go a long way in not only easing their fears, but beginning the process of open communication and understanding.

Third: you need to know the limits. There are going to be some boundaries—which will still need to be stated—that might truly need some conditioning for your parents or authority figures to begin understanding or accepting them. This is where the grace that was previously talked about, comes in. For most of us, our parents want us to live a happy, thriving and successful life. Unfortunately, a lot of our conflicts come through the clashing of how they view that life versus how we intend to live it. Establishing and maintaining open communication about these things will go a long way in being able to respect your own boundaries and theirs. Sometimes you, or your parents/authority figures, will need to take a step back to gain clarity and space. This is natural and healthy, and while it may freak some people out due to personality, conflict resolution, or past traumas, do not rush this process. Forcing someone to accept your boundaries by constantly harassing them through the guise of open communication is not fair, and a good way to breed resentment. On the same side, you being able to tell your parents you need some space to think things through and gather your thoughts alerts them to the fact that not only have you matured enough to understand when you need time to think; it will also give you the ability to regroup and reconfigure how you are going to ensure that this boundary is respected.

As Parents

Alright, so many things were said to the adult children. Now it is time for the parents. As parents, there are going to be many times when your children will want a certain thing that you wish they did not—such as those body modifications, or less than ideal living situations. However, there are several things to remember: the first is that if they are legally of age, there is not a lot you can do if it is not under your roof. And no, you cannot keep them under your roof if they do not want to stay.

What this also means is that, just like your child, you still have a right to your own boundaries and house rules. Do not let your child sway you otherwise, unless it is something you truly believe needs to be swayed.

However, there is another aspect of setting boundaries with adult children that needs to be discussed:

implementing stronger boundaries if your adult child is taking advantage of you. Before you get up in arms saying, "They are my child, they can't take advantage of me!" begin to think about their life circumstances, what you are currently doing, and how involved in their lives you actually are. It is one thing if your child is a student and you are occasionally helping financially because that was either the deal, or they are struggling. What is really being discussed here, are the adult children who are still coddled like a child. This is going to hurt to hear, but if that is you and your child, you are enabling them to live an irresponsible life.

While that statement might seem a bit heavy-handed, remember, you are the parent. Meaning no one knows the boundaries and expectations in play better than you. Once you realize the value of your own boundaries, you can start to see the difference between if they actually need help, versus them just wanting to be lazy and you're just making life too easy for them. It might be time for them to learn some hard truths.

So how do you set those boundaries?

According to Allison Bottke, there are several easy steps to begin setting your own boundaries to ensure that both you and your child are living a boundary-healthy life: stop swooping in, gather a support group, immediately stop excuses, implement your own boundaries and respect them, trust your instincts (you have raised them this long, it is time to see if that gut instinct is still in tact) and yield to the understanding that you fixing everything will not ensure your child's long-term success, (Bottke, 2022/2019).

Setting Boundaries With Siblings

Alright, so with parental and authority figures out of the way, it is time to consider boundaries with siblings. Similar to parental/authority figures, your siblings live with you for a certain period of your life, meaning that they most likely know, or have a good idea, of what your boundaries already are. The problem then, is because your sibling intrinsically knows your boundaries—but does not know the specifics since they most likely have not been told what the boundary actually is—things can get lost in translation and the enactment of understanding. But, let's not forget that this is discussing siblings. Which means that miscommunication and misunderstandings run high, as well as quick and easy tempers, ignorance, and the deliberate choice of ignorance in some situations.

Thankfully, enforcing and beginning to establish boundaries with your siblings, like with your parents, boils down to several key habits that you are already aware of. Clearly communicating your boundaries, respecting your own boundaries, and having fail-safe plans in place for when your sibling does not respect your boundaries (starting a fight or confrontation does not count).

Now, another thing that could be useful in regards to siblings could be finding a safe person to be your mediator when tempers run, so high that there is no way you would be able to clearly communicate through it.

Before closing off the family section there is a tiny caveat that should be discussed: Just because they are your family does not mean that they should be given the extension of grace constantly when they willingly choose to ignore or not recognize your boundaries. The saying "blood is thicker than water" should not extend towards your personal safety, or your mental, physical or spiritual well-being. All of which are defined, communicated, and enforced through the enactment and respect of your boundaries.

With Friends

Boundaries with friends are pretty similar to boundaries with siblings, except with one crucial difference: Your friends may not know you as well as your siblings, because they most likely have not lived with you, or known you for that long. Which then means that you have to really up your communication game to ensure that your friends respect your boundaries. And that means being prepared to have uncomfortable talks, if necessary.

For instance, say you have two friends: James and Mike. You have known them for a few years and they have always pushed you outside of your comfort zone, but in good ways. They encouraged you when you were scared, but also challenged you to do things you would not normally do. When you tell them your limits, they respect them, and help you either work through them (if it is a fear-based problem you want to confront), or help you find solutions if it is something you are unwilling to change. They listen to you when you say that it is a hard limit and you are uncomfortable. And they also ask you questions on when you want to be pushed, and when you do not.

Notice how James and Mike ensured that communication was the foundation for how they respect your boundaries, as well as encouraged you to do things you were scared to do (remember the myth of saying no). This type of open communication and respect of boundaries is what you should strive for in your friendships and boundaries.

Setting Boundaries in Romantic Relationships

Boundaries in romantic relationships are both easy and

difficult. They are easy because they are discussed more frequently, and more people are willing to put effort into maintaining those types of boundaries. They are also difficult because they involve being vulnerable with someone you most likely want to keep in your life, but that vulnerability comes at the cost of baring your soul and being willing to communicate about it. On top of that, there is the added problem of what was discussed in the first chapter: your happiness, wants, and needs, are not necessarily your partners' full-time job. Yes, they should be aiming to make you happy and to meet your wants and needs, but they are not solely responsible for them. You are.

Remember: Your boundaries are what *you* are responsible for. So, if one of your wants in the relationship is to have good communication, it is not fair—or right—for you to expect that of your partner, but then you yourself do not engage or communicate regularly.

So then, how do you ensure that your wants and needs are taken care of, while your boundaries are respected? Easy. Communicate with your partner, and be responsible (Gilles, n.d.). Sounds too good to be true, right? Well, you are not entirely wrong. Communicating with your partner—as many probably know—takes a lot of effort. But it is honestly worth the effort. Proper communication eliminates any guess work on your end as you have established that it is okay for you to ask questions and validate what you believe they are thinking or feeling in a given scenario (with the footnote that you are okay to be wrong and to be gently corrected).

Additionally, taking responsibility will lift a huge weight off of the pressure of a relationship, as well as the additional pressure of maintaining boundaries in a relationship, because you are straight up owning your responsibilities in the relationship (like your choices, your emotions, and your actions). Being proactive and taking ownership will save you numerous fights as well as begin to establish the enactment of healthy boundaries.

At Work

Depending on where you work, boundaries at work may not be an issue at all. Or perhaps it is one of the more impossible sections of this book. Part of the reason why boundaries at work seem so impossible is because we believe that if something is given to us, we have to jump immediately to solve or accomplish that task, leading to long days, few moments of rest, and a feeling like we are drowning under the corporate pile of never-ending paperwork and training seminars.

But it does not have to be that way.

Thankfully, most companies actually do have systems in place (or they are putting them in place) to help you build better boundaries, except it is not phrased that way. Often, when confronting work boundaries—or the lack thereof —the key word that is used is 'burnout', because the results are the same. Having no boundaries at work results in you taking on so much more than you can handle, which leads to you being burned out. One of the best solutions to burnout is to begin communicating your boundaries clearly and being proactive before things and projects escalate out of control.

However, there are several things that go into this boundary implementation plan, a lot of which include you doing some deep soul-searching.

Work Journaling

Alright, so, first off, take a moment with your journal and begin to ask yourself the following hard questions:

What am I actually responsible for in this position? What do I feel responsible for?

Then, really sit there and begin to think about how different those two lists are (if they are not, but you are still feeling like your boundaries are not being respected at work, do not worry, we will get there).

Often, when identifying where our boundaries are going awry in places like the workplace, we have to begin separating what we are actually responsible for, versus what we think we are being asked to accomplish; the overstepping of our boundaries are often found in the differences between those lists.

If you notice a difference, set up a meeting with your boss and begin to discuss that difference specifically. For that meeting you should not only have those two lists, but also have what you make a priority for your role (which should include your understanding of the role so far). Additionally, go into that meeting being prepared to negotiate your tasks and what will be required of you, but ensure that it is honestly what you can handle in a workday.

Now, if you do not notice that type of discrepancy (or even if you do), begin to look at the reasons why you might be feeling overwhelmed, specifically by looking at your day and journaling/writing down what is causing you stress and anxiety. Is it because your coworkers take up too much of your time? Is it because your inbox gets way too full? Is it because you need help but do not want to ask? When working on a team with multiple people, being sure of your boundaries is a key practice to success, but somewhere along the line, we forgot that boundaries include being okay to ask for help, or referring to other people, or even—gasp—delegating when we actually cannot complete something.

Somehow, modern society has taken the concept of pushing ourselves to the limit to pushing ourselves closer to the brink of insanity, rather than ensuring that we, and others, actually excel. Confused about how the two paragraphs link up? Let's walk it through from the beginning. Your boundaries are what you can or cannot handle and what you will or will not be responsible for. And somewhere along the line, you forgot to ensure that those boundaries were respected at work because you are now feeling overwhelmed, overworked, and probably underappreciated and over stressed. So, then, where are those boundaries going wrong?

They are either going wrong in your lack of communicating your boundaries or maintaining them, your lack of refusal to delegate your workload to honor your boundaries and your lack or inability to say no and set limits. As mentioned multiple times throughout this book: Saying no, as long as it is not refusing your actual job or what is expected of you, is not a bad thing. And if you have somehow worked yourself into a corner where you have taken on too much and cannot necessarily back out easily, schedule a talk with your manager and be honest. Most managers (again, not all, this would be something that you would know better) appreciate honesty. If you admit you made a mistake, but are able to show your proactivity by bringing a list of how you will not do this again, admitting you made a mistake should technically not be a black mark on your record within that company.

Online

This section is a little new, but in our increasingly technological-based world it is very important to begin to figure out what your boundaries will be with any type of media. These boundaries specifically involve the question of: what you will or will not share and tolerate online.

For instance, will it be okay for you to have a public account and invite anyone and everyone to see, like, and comment on your photos? Including the trolls?

Additionally, are you being appropriate for the platform and the type of account you have created? Influencers aside, it is rarely seen as appropriate to overshare your personal life on a business account, yet so many people do it. Which results in blurred boundaries and a poor enactment of what your responsibilities—for a professional account—are.

To set good online boundaries, seriously consider the platform and account. Think about what you want those things to represent, and which aspect of your life they align with. Create several different accounts if that is what it takes, but ensure that your boundaries are firm and well thought out here, because what goes online will never go away (Castrillon, 2019).

Journaling

That was a lot of information, so again, feel free to re-read this chapter and highlight or take notes on anything you specifically want to focus on going forward.

Before going forward, really look at each life relationship and begin to plot out where certain relationships of yours could use with some boundary strengthening. Look at the examples and strategies given and use those to create your own plan.

Chapter 5

Life With Boundaries

While it sounds repetitive, it cannot be overstated: Life with boundaries is so much simpler and easier to deal with.

Hopefully by now you have a pretty good idea of what your boundaries are, how you are going to enforce them, where you are lacking boundaries, and how you are going to begin re-enforcing them.

However, before completely ending the talk on boundaries, we still have to consider what your life will look like with them, specifically through a few things that you have been promised would be discussed and have not been yet. These areas include how to handle those who are going to ignore your boundaries and what your duty is going forward.

Confronting the Ignorant

Sadly, there will still be people who ignore your boundaries. And there is not much you can do about it. If the relationship is important to you, you can try to communicate with them, get a mediator or therapist to join those conversations, and come up with game plans together. But at the end of the day, if they do not put in the effort to respect your boundaries, you may have to be okay with distancing yourself from that relationship.

While it sounds harsh, there is nothing worse for you—especially right now—than being close to someone who is not going to respect your boundaries. Embarking on this journey is going to be hard, and it is going to require so much consistency that having a large cheer squad to help you through it is honestly almost a requirement. Since this journey is going to be that hard (anything that requires consistency does), having even one close negative influence might be enough to persuade you to stop.

Do not let that happen. You have done so much of the ground work already, do not stop now.

If that was not enough to sway you, consider this: The people who are ignoring your boundaries are probably one of the main reasons (as long as you are communicating and doing the groundwork discussed so far) you may feel like your boundaries are not being met. Most people are highly aware of when their boundaries are not being met, but many will give their relationships the benefit of the doubt—as they should. Perhaps you were not clear enough, perhaps they misunderstood, perhaps they forgot. All of these potential circumstances are more than possible, but it is your duty to figure out if they are reality.

If they are not, then not only is that relationship deliberately ignoring something you need, but you have already picked up on it. And if you have already picked up on it and are noticing the negative effects of that, why are you fighting to stay?

What Goes Around Comes Around

Once more: Your boundaries are yours alone, and they deserve respect.

However, if you expect other people to respect your boundaries, you have to reciprocate. It is incredibly selfish of you to expect everyone else to know, remember, and respect your boundaries while you completely walk all over someone else's.

Boundaries are built on communication, yes, but also on mutual respect.

Conclusion

And with that, we have reached the end of our book on boundaries. Hopefully you are more than prepared and eager to continue on your boundary journey. As you continue, remember several things:

- It will be hard, but worth it.

- You need to be consistent.

- Communication is key.

- The myths are called 'myths' for a reason.

- You are worthy of your boundaries being respected in every relationship you come across.

- Boundaries work on a reciprocal rule.

If you ever feel like this journey is too much for you, reach out to a safe person. It is completely okay if you cannot do this alone. Even if you need a cheering squad, ask someone for it, and know that so many people are cheering you on to begin your healthy boundary journey.

Thank You

Before you leave, I'd just like to say, thank you so much for purchasing my book.

I spent many days and nights working on this book so I could finally put this in your hands.

So, before you leave, I'd like to ask you a small favor.

Would you please consider posting a review on the platform? Your reviews are one of the best ways to support indie authors like me, and every review counts.

Your feedback will allow me to continue writing books just like this one, so let me know if you enjoyed it and why. I read every review and I would love to hear from you.

To leave a review simply scan these QR codes below or go to Amazon, go to "Your Orders" and then find it under "Orders".

amazon.com   amazon.co.uk

References

Blundell, A. (2019, June 25). *12 signs you lack healthy boundaries (and why you need them)*. Harley Therapy Blog. https://www.harleytherapy.co.uk/counselling/healthy-boundaries.htm

Bottke, A. (2019). *Setting Boundaries with your adult children: Six steps to hope and healing for struggling parents*. Harvest House Publishers. (Original work published 2022)

Campbell, L. (2021, June 8). *Personal boundaries: Types and how to set them*. (B. Juby, Ed.). PsychCentral. https://psychcentral.com/lib/what-are-personal-boundaries-how-do-i-get-some

Castrillon, C. (2019, July 18). *10 ways to set healthy boundaries at work*. Forbes. https://www.forbes.com/sites/carolinecastrillon/2

019/07/18/10-ways-to-set-healthy-boundaries-at-work/?sh=5e98e10c7497

Cloud, H., & John Sims Townsend. (1995). *Safe people: How to find relationships that are good for you and avoid those that aren't.* Zondervan Pub. House. (Original work published 2022)

Cloud, H., & John Sims Townsend. (2002). *Boundaries: When to say yes, how to say no, to take control of your life.* Zondervan Pub. House.

Daino, J. (2022, February 4). *How to set family boundaries: A therapist's guide.* (C. Catchings, Ed.). Talkspace. https://www.talkspace.com/blog/family-boundaries/

Earnshaw, E. (2019, July 20). *6 Types of boundaries you deserve to have (and how to maintain them).* MindBodyGreen. https://www.mindbodygreen.com/articles/six-types-of-boundaries-and-what-healthy-boundaries-look-like-for-each

Gilles, G. (n.d.). *The importance of boundaries in romantic relationships.* MentalHelp.net. Retrieved March 31, 2022, from https://www.mentalhelp.net/blogs/the-importance-of-boundaries-in-romantic-relationships/

References

McLaughlin, M. (2000, January 23). *Boundaries and how to use them: Based off of dr. Henry Cloud and John Townsend's book "Boundaries"*. [Slides].

Merriam-Webster. (n.d.). *Grace*. Merriam-Webster. Retrieved March 30, 2022, from https://www.merriam-webster.com/dictionary/grace

Merriam-Webster. (2022). *People pleaser*. Merriam-Webster. https://www.merriam-webster.com/dictionary/people%20pleaser

Mort, S. (2021, May 16). *Are boundaries selfish? The answer is more complicated than you think*. Dr. Soph. https://drsoph.com/blog/are-boundaries-selfish-or-controlling

Pattemore, C. (2021, June 3). *10 ways to build and preserve better boundaries*. (J. Johnson, Ed.). Psych Central. https://psychcentral.com/lib/10-way-to-build-and-preserve-better-boundaries#what-are-boundaries

Risser, M. (2021, October 4). *11 ways to practice emotional self care*. Choosing Therapy. https://www.choosingtherapy.com/emotional-self-care/

Selva, J. (2018, January 5). *How to set healthy boundaries: 10 examples + pdf worksheets*. PositivePsychology.com.

https://positivepsychology.com/great-self-care-setting-healthy-boundaries/

Tartakovsky, M. (2019, March 4). *A pep talk for people pleasers for setting boundaries.* (Scientific Advisory Board, Ed.). Psych Central. https://psychcentral.com/lib/a-pep-talk-for-people-pleasers-for-setting-boundaries#6

theoffcamerashow. (2021, January 8). *WandaVision's Elizabeth Olsen: "No" is a full sentence.* Www.youtube.com. https://www.youtube.com/watch?v=Lev9zK5JWvg

Vigliotti, A. (2020, December 10). *3 biggest myths about boundaries.* Psychology Today. https://www.psychologytoday.com/ca/blog/the-now/202012/3-biggest-myths-about-boundaries

Virro, K. (2020, August 24). *Harmful myths about boundaries.* Fresh Insight. https://www.fresh-insight.ca/post/harmful-myths-about-boundaries

Printed in Great Britain
by Amazon